MAKING EFFECTI'

Some other titles in this series

Building Self-Esteem	Manage a Sales Team
Career Networking	Manage an Office
Career Planning for Women	Manage Computers at Work
Communicate at Work	Manage Your Career
Conducting Effective Interviews	Managing Meetings
Conducting Effective Negotiations	Managing Projects
Conducting Staff Appraisals	Managing Successful Teams
Controlling Anxiety	Mastering Business English
Coping with Self Assessment	Mastering Public Speaking
Counsel People at Work	Maximising Your Memory
Creating a Web Site	Organising Effective Training
Delivering Customer Service	Starting to Manage
Do Your Own Advertising	Staying Ahead at Work
Do Your Own PR	Taking on Staff
Doing Business Abroad	Thriving on Stress
Doing Business on the Internet	Unlocking Your Potential
Employ and Manage Staff	Using the Internet
Finding a Job with a Future	Winning Presentations
Investing in People	Work in an Office
Know Your Rights at Work	Write a Press Release
Learning New Job Skills	Writing a Report
Making a Wedding Speech	Writing Business Letters

Other titles in preparation

The How To Series now contains nearly 250 titles in the following categories:

Business & Management	Personal Finance
Computer Basics	Self-Development
General Reference	Small Business
Jobs & Careers	Student Handbooks
Living & Working Abroad	Successful Writing

Please send for a free copy of the latest catalogue for full details (see back cover for address).

BUSINESS & MANAGEMENT

MAKING EFFECTIVE SPEECHES

How to motivate and persuade in
every business situation

John Bowden

How To Books

By the same author in this series:

Making a Wedding Speech
Writing a Report

Cartoons by Mike Flanagan

British Library Cataloguing in Publication Data
A catalogue record for this book is available from the British Library.

First published by How To Books Ltd, 3 Newtec Place,
Magdalen Road, Oxford, OX4 1RE, United Kingdom.
Tel: (01865) 793806. Fax: (01865) 248780.
email: info@howtobooks.co.uk
www.howtobooks.co.uk

Note: The material contained in this book is set out in good faith for general
guidance and no liability can be accepted for loss or expense incurred as a result of
relying in particular circumstances on statements made in the book. The laws and
regulations are complex and liable to change, and readers should check the current
position with the relevant authorities before making personal arrangements.

Produced for How To Books by Deer Park Productions.
Typeset by Anneset, Weston-super-Mare, North Somerset.
Printed and bound by Cromwell Press, Trowbridge, Wiltshire.

Contents

List of Illustrations

Preface

All over the world thousands, perhaps tens of thousands of business speeches are made every day – at conferences, workshops, seminars, symposiums, meetings. The list of functions at which people may be speaking is endless. Business executives find themselves planted on platforms, before microphones; forced onto TV or radio; selling before prospective clients or customers; pitching for orders or work; enthusing, encouraging or rallying their colleagues, managers or sales force. Success in business today does not happen by chance and effective speeches are not made by accident.

This is *not* a book for individuals who want to control their nerves as they stand up and speak to an audience. You'll find plenty of less ambitious titles that will help you achieve this. Nor is it for those who wish to join the legions of coached speakers who apparently *want* to look and sound the same as one another. You will not be bombarded with tuition and theory or put in a straitjacket of techniques that will stifle your individuality and unique personality.

This book is addressed to every executive who wants to take that giant leap in effectiveness by learning how to *add value* to their speeches through the successful transfer of skills, creation of awareness or provision of enjoyment. What we shall be tackling is more than *public* speaking, it is *professional* speaking. Public speakers aim to give an audience what they believe it *wants*; professional speakers give it what they know it *needs*. Public speakers judge success by clapometer readings; professional speakers judge it by the degree to which *objectives* are met, or preferably exceeded. To a professional speaker, outcome is all. This book is addressed to speakers who want to get results.

The use of masculine nouns and pronouns throughout the text stems from my desire to avoid ugly, cumbersome English, and reflects the fact that the majority of business executives are still male. No discrimination, prejudice or bias is intended.

John Bowden

9

1
Deciding Whether or Not to Speak

Would your organisation spend anything between £5,000 and £10,000 on an unnecessary piece of equipment? Almost certainly not. Would your organisation spend a similar sum on an unnecessary speech? Quite possibly it would.

Companies rarely even consider costs or value for money of making a speech to an internal audience – and they find it difficult to set a realistic fee for an external one. Why? Probably because a speech is intangible. Yet the hidden costs are considerable: administrative costs, secretarial costs, opportunity costs, travel and subsistence costs; time in cars, taxis, and possibly trains and boats and planes. When you tally it all up, it can come to a great deal of money and time. And time is the limiting factor for most executives.

To speak or not to speak? Before you accept an invitation to address an external audience, or prepare yourself to address an internal one, you must ask yourself some critical questions. The decision involves some major considerations: the audience's needs, your ability to satisfy them, your organisation's objectives, and your time and availability. It requires a balanced judgement that should be made intelligently.

ESTABLISHING THE AUDIENCE'S NEEDS

People who address audiences have the potential to create tremendous value – or create tremendous harm.

> **The only reason to make a speech is to improve the condition of the audience and, frequently, the organisations which they represent.**

That improvement may come from the transfer of skills, the initiation of immediate action, the awareness of a condition, the provocation of their emotions, the interactions among them, or the appreciation of their potential.

Audiences know what they *want*. Speakers know what they *need* – or they should do. If they do not, they must find out. The mere act of exploring, understanding and clarifying your precise objectives will add enormous value to your contribution. The status quo is not the desire or there would be no need for a speech. What outcome do you want? What changes do you require in the audience's attitudes and behaviour? By what standard will you judge success?

Concentrating on the objective

The more you concentrate on **objectives** and desired **outcomes**, the more valuable you are going to be. The more you focus on the associated events and tasks, the more vulnerable you become. Delivering a motivational speech is not an objective, it is a *task*. The *objective* may be to challenge participants to achieve higher goals. When considering whether or not to speak, concentrate on the intended objective, not the associated task. Here are some other examples of tasks translated into possible objectives:

Task	Objective
• Conducting sales training	• Improving sales closing rates
• Delivering a keynote speech	• Creating a need to listen and learn
• Teaching interpersonal skills	• Reducing conflict at work
• Discussing stress reduction.	• Improving productivity.

Value-added must be considered in terms of some output, some result, some bettered position. At this stage, do not think about what you could *say*, think about what *beneficial effect* you could produce. What could be different and better after three weeks, three months, three years?

MATCHING YOUR PROCESS SKILLS

Too many speakers restrict their speaking engagements to ones relating directly to areas of personal experience or subject knowledge. This is short-sighted. The key is to recognise that skills and abilities are transferable. It is important to distinguish between **content** and **process**:

– A **process** is a sequence, system, design, model, or approach that enables the user to achieve a given, desired result. For example, a sales process may allow a salesperson to more quickly and efficiently generate new business.

– **Content** is the particular environment, surroundings, subject matter or specifics within which processes are applied. The sales process at Nissan involves selling cars, but at Zurich it involves selling insurance. Yet the basic process skills of selling are the same, whether you are selling cars, insurance – or widgets.

The following are examples of the many processes that are applicable to a vast array of people, places, organisations and conditions. Do any of *your* broad process skills match the *audience's* needs?

- leadership
- image building
- priority setting
- marketing
- creativity
- media skills
- problem solving
- technological skills
- planning
- customer care
- time management

- managing change
- sales skills
- productivity
- career development
- motivation
- health and safety
- building self-esteem
- team building
- networking
- IT skills
- communications.

If they do, it will be straightforward to build content and context around them. If they do not, it is better not to speak.

CONSIDERING PERSONAL PROS AND CONS

It is useful to distinguish between the two basic categories of business speech: ones to internal and external audiences – and then to consider the advantages and potential difficulties associated with each.

Addressing internal audiences

The vast majority of speeches fall into this category, for example addressing or briefing groups of staff; presenting a case to a management committee or board; introducing plans; reporting back, or giving thanks to colleagues. Here are some factors that may help and some that may hinder a speech made within your own organisation:

Internal audiences

Advantages

- Easy to define desired outcome.

- Easy to monitor medium- and long-term results.

- Often share process and content skills with audience.

- Rapport with staff.

- Greater experience and knowledge than staff.

- More authority than staff.

- Familiarity with rooms.

- Access to equipment.

- Access to technical support.

- Knowledge of audience.

- Known to the audience.

Potential difficulties

- Preconceived ideas about the audience.

- Complacency.

- Audience has preconceived ideas about you.

- Need to comply with 'house rules' and conventions.

- Peers can be competitive and hostile.

- May be inter-departmental rivalry.

The most important advantage is *knowledge*. Your inside information should give you a clear and detailed picture of what you need to achieve and how best you can do so.

Addressing external audiences

The range of external speeches will often be far greater than those within your organisation, for example, speaking at conferences; or talking to meetings of public, special interests, community groups, councillors, professional bodies or trades unions. They have a different set of personal advantages and potential difficulties. Let us consider some of them:

External audiences

Advantages
- Useful for personal development.

- May have fewer preconceived ideas about the audience.

- Audience may have fewer preconceived ideas about you.

- Higher interest and motivation.

- May have access to more facilities and equipment.

Potential difficulties
- May prove difficult to establish the audience's precise needs.

- Will be difficult to monitor medium- and long-term results.

- May be unaware of their concerns and pressures.

- May need to build content and context around shared process skills.

- Lack of familiarity with the audience.

- Lack of familiarity about the venue and so on.

- May need extra preparation time.

- Practical difficulties, such as long distance travel.

Most experienced speakers would agree that external presentations have far more potential problems and most of these stem from *a lack of knowledge*.

With internal audiences, knowledge is often the main advantage. With external audiences it is the main potential difficulty.

Balancing the personal pros and cons
Try to develop a clear picture of precisely what is involved. Consider the advantages and disadvantages, including all the personal commitment that would be necessary. Only you can decide how much time you would need for preparation:

- How important is the speech?

- How heavy is your current workload?

- How familiar are you with the general process?

- How familiar are you with the specific content?

- How much new preparation would be needed?

- How much time could you allow for this?

- Would you have to postpone other aspects of your work?

- Is there anything happening at home or at work that could interfere with your preparation?

- How often will you need to be out of your workplace over the next few days or weeks?

- Would anyone help you do the research?

- Would anyone help you prepare your high- or low-tech audio-visual material?

- Could you get easy access to the material you require?

The questions go on and on, but they all boil down to this: What's in it for you and is it worth all the time and effort? Rightly or wrongly, people think that if you make a good speech, you are good at your job and, conversely, if you make a bad speech you are poor at it. This may not be fair or even reasonable, but it happens. Perception is reality. There is no response other than to be highly selective about the speeches you choose to deliver and then to maximise their impact.

> **By putting on a professional show you can positively and actively build your image and increase the chances of acceptance of anything that you are promoting.**

This is true with both internal or external audiences. It is a fact that no potential speaker can afford to forget.

CONSIDERING CORPORATE PROS AND CONS

As a speaker, you must always consider the importance and value of a speech to the organisation you represent – the organisation that pays your salary. Routine and less important speeches can often be presented by junior members of staff. However, there will be times when it is necessary for senior speakers to address specific audiences, perhaps to show how seriously the organisation takes the central message of the speech, or perhaps to add some gravitas to the occasion. Here are some typical reasons why it may be in the interests of an organisation for an executive to speak:

- To set company policy.
- To establish an image.
- To (re-)establish a personal bond with an audience.
- To influence important decisions.
- To attract media and public attention.
- To explain the importance of organisational change.

To set company policy
Speeches have always provided the occasion to espouse company policy. Because keynote speeches are recorded, and often written or at least transcribed, they can serve as a permanent record of company policy that can guide other executives and personnel as they attempt to accurately represent the company in public. Additionally such speeches can help set the tone, direction and values of the corporation. Delivered in public settings – often amplified with media presence – speeches can set the agenda for organisational policy and culture.

To establish an image
What sort of image would your organisation like to project: businesslike, authoritative, open, friendly, caring? A speech can help establish this image. We all know of some executive who is sought after as a speaker. His audience may know next to nothing about his organisation, but when he starts talking, they listen. He is conversational. He projects his personality. Everyone can understand each point he makes. He keeps them interested in what he is going to say next and, every now and then, he scores a comfortable laugh. He oozes confidence. When he sits down, that audience will regard his organisation differently. The company and what it does will have become a more familiar and friendlier part of life. This is a fact, not fancy. Every accomplished communicator in the world of business knows it to be true.

To (re-)establish a personal bond with an audience
Companies and organisations will always need to establish personal

links with specific audiences. While we talk of *companies* doing business with other *companies*, in reality, of course, it is *people* who are doing business with other *people*. Perhaps there has been a rift in the past. Maybe there never has been a strong tie and now, because of changing times, one is necessary. Whatever the reason, companies can solidify linkages with audiences by proving they have a human face. A personal emissary can (re-)open channels of communication, thereby overcoming years of possible hostility or misunderstandings.

To influence important decisions
In the real world, more often than we may like to believe, narrow decisions can come down to a primitive tribal acclamation of an individual. This may well be based on the impression made during the course of a speech. Successful organisations recognise this and encourage their most charismatic executives to address their most important audiences. They know, quite simply, that close decisions can hang on whether an audience likes and respects someone or not. The irrational starts to take over from the rational. Feelings take over from arguments. Emotion takes over from logic. People still talk about objective criteria but they now use them not to reach a rational conclusion, but to justify an irrational one. The audience may not know this, and it certainly will never admit it, but the right personal chemistry really can tip the balance in your favour.

To attract media and public attention
A speech is an ideal way for an organisation to promote news, real or apparent. The media is always looking for something interesting and quotable to report. Whether you are opening a new office, creating new jobs, launching a new product or unveiling a research project of public interest, tell them about it. A speech is an excellent way to put yourself, your organisation and your product in the public eye.

To explain the importance of organisational change
Change in the businessworld is now fundamental to success and progress. Adaptation to the increasing pressures which organisations, individuals and teams are facing in the workplace is essential. A speech by an executive will keep people aware of what is happening, and why it is happening. It can be the lubricant of change. It will also provide the key feedback mechanism whereby organisations find out what is really happening with their customers, with their quality

programmes and with the way their employees are taking the business forward.

Communicating directly

Most successful organisations are becoming increasingly employee-centred. Senior managers are beginning to realise that in order to run their companies effectively, they have to come out of their offices and communicate directly with their staff, just as generals have to leave their tents on the battlefield and talk to their troops, and politicians have to get out of their ivory towers and tell people in the street what it is they intend to achieve and how they intend to achieve it.

MAKING THE DECISION

The bottom line is: Is this speech worth making? Are the hours of preparation, the costs, time away from the office, worth the probable personal and corporate gains? These may sound cold and callous questions, but they have to be asked. Speeches, like widgets, cost money.

Employing a corporate speechwriter

You may have concluded that while it is worth making this speech, you simply do not have enough time to prepare it. This can become a more and more pressing problem as you move up the corporate ladder. The difficulty is compounded by the fact that generally you will be addressing higher-level audiences than before and the importance of getting everything just right becomes more crucial than ever, and seemingly more difficult to achieve.

Unused, underused or misused writing talent is all too common in large corporations. Perhaps your advertising copywriters, house magazine feature writers, or public relations director or press and publicity officer, possess the skills necessary for writing good speeches. Perhaps all they need is a briefing on the message you want to convey, a copy of this book and the chance to have a go. Don't give well intentioned aides the opportunity to blue-pencil every trace of daring and dash from their draft. Read it aloud. Tape it and play it back. Does it capture your personality and natural style as a speaker? Its faults and virtues will reveal themselves immediately.

Calling in the professionals

If you cannot find a suitable writer from within your organisation, aside from personal recommendation from successful corporate speakers or top executives you trust, you might consider approaching a speech writing service company. Their fees are high but their experts understand the subtleties of spoken persuasion and their best writers can put your voice into print. Your speeches will be given that unique tone that is recognisably yours, and only yours.

Putting it all into perspective

Many major companies are at last beginning to realise that the effectiveness of their spoken communication is a strategic issue, something that has to be addressed at the highest levels of management before it can work at every other level. Speeches are important, very important. They must succeed. Or rather, *you* must make them succeed.

The decision whether or not to speak is critical. A well-prepared and appropriate 30-minute speech to an audience can do wonders for you and your organisation. A poorly-prepared or inappropriate 30-minute speech to 200 people may waste only half an hour of your time, but will waste 100 hours of their time – more than 12 working days. That should be a hanging offence.

The content of the remainder of this book is based on the assumption that you have decided that on this occasion it *is* worth making a speech – and, that *you* will be the one who prepares and presents it.

QUESTIONS AND ANSWERS

Under what circumstances is a written report a more appropriate medium of communication than a speech, and vice versa?

The written word has many powers, and in many cases is a far more time-efficient way of transferring *information*, particularly if it is lengthy or detailed. Yet reports and memoranda can never be as effective as speeches as a means of conveying an important *message* in a succinct, powerful and memorable way. Most people can remember things said by Sir Winston Churchill, Dr Martin Luther King and JFK, but very few of us can recall anything they wrote.

Far too many business people still believe that if they have something really important to communicate to a target group, they should *always* put it in writing. They have been conditioned by an educational system heavily weighted towards the visual and literary. Yet if they stopped to think about their own reading habits they would realise just how few written messages aimed at them actually get read at all. And of those that are read, most are skimmed through and are soon forgotten, however important they may have seemed at the time. If they looked back over their lives, they would remember the essence of many important things *said* to them, and key messages and moments would be firmly implanted in their brains.

By providing a living, breathing person to speak rather than sending a sterile report or memorandum an organisation is saying: This is *important*. Something needs to done. So long as it is not overused, a speech can 'make a difference'.

Can a speaker's value ever be based solely upon expert content knowledge?

Certainly, and there are many such specialist speakers out there: experts in the fine points of the law, financial operations, chemical analysis and so on. However, if you position yourself as a content expert, by definition you severely restrict your potential field of operation. And you had better be good. The value-added of content experts can only be better content knowledge: how they can build that better mousetrap.

If comedy is such a serious business, should I be wary of accepting an invitation to give an entertainment speech?

Humour is an essential ingredient in any successful business speech. It makes the audience relax and listen to your serious message. You don't need to tell jokes; a sprinkling of relevant amusing anecdotes here and there is often more effective. Your humour should be spread thinly like caviar, not piled on like marmalade.

The problem with making an entertainment speech is that you are *expected* to be funny *throughout*, and while humour is universal, taste in humour is individual. Devotees of *Terry and June* may be less than impressed by *Monty Python's Flying Circus*, and vice versa. Knowing the audience's culture and background will help a speaker hit the mark more directly. A good place to employ a speech to entertain is with an audience you know well: an internal audience. Certainly it is appropriate at a retirement or corporate party to inject humour, but in this case you, as speaker, have the inside story and know the culture. But with an unknown audience, use caution. Leave such speeches to their insiders or to professional entertainers.

CASE STUDIES

Sophie does a little lateral thinking

Sophie is a management consultant. Using the analogy of how difficult it is for athletes to remain competitive once they become detached from the leading pack in a middle or long distance race, she has built a solid reputation as a speaker who can help organisations *avoid* dangerous gaps developing between themselves and market leaders. When she receives an invitation to address one of these front-runners, her first reaction is to ask herself what possible value she could add to their business. Why would they want to know how to avoid gaps developing? On the contrary. . . This gives her the idea to re-work her speech to tell the 'big boys how to *create* and maintain gaps between themselves and the also-rans. She accepts the engagement.

Keith goes on air

Keith is the chairman of a car manufacturing company. When his company acquires a fellow car manufacturer, Keith decides that he should speak to the new combined dealer network. His objective is to tell them exactly what is going on in order to avoid rumours developing. His problem is how to address a geographically diverse audience without unnecessary delay. His solution is business television, arguably the most powerful and cost effective medium for driving information through a business. Within 18 hours the entire dealer network is watching a detailed behind-the-scenes briefing. There are no Chinese whispers and no trickle-down, only direct communication between Keith and his dealers. The transition goes very smoothly. Keith's desired outcome has been realised.

James gets out the camcorder

James is a director of a publisher-broadcast company which has taken over an English TV franchise. He needs to explain to the new workforce of 350 the changes that are to take place: revised conditions of service, different ways of supplying programmes to the network, different ways of making regional programmes. He decides that he should speak to them directly. It is not practicable for them to get together at any particular place and time, and James cannot afford the time that would be necessary for him to travel round the region to meet them. His answer is to address them through a series of five-minute video modules that can be mixed and matched according to the requirements of various groups of workers. He sees two main advantages to this strategy. First, the various presentations can be run by different executives without any inconsistency of approach. Second, workers who see the same modules will receive identical messages. By the time the company goes on air 15 months later, all staff have been apprised of the changes and how they affect them.

SUMMARY

- Are the needs of the potential audience clear and attainable?

- Have you established precisely what outcome, result or better position is required?

- Could *you* achieve and preferably exceed this desired outcome?

- Is a speech the most appropriate medium?

- Is it necessary for *you* to prepare the speech?

- Is it necessary for *you* to deliver the speech?

- Is it worthwhile for you?

- Is it worthwhile for your organisation?

- On balance, is it worth it?

2
Taking an Overview

Once you have made the decision to speak to a particular group, the real work starts. Like the journey of a thousand miles, it must begin with the first step: an overview of what you intend to achieve, and how you intend to achieve it. This chapter will help you take that essential overview. Specifically it will cover:

- focusing on the desired outcome
- analysing the audience
- relating desired outcome to audience
- remaining on-message
- putting the right slant on it.

FOCUSING ON THE DESIRED OUTCOME

Every speech should have an outcome. A lecture on investment strategy should maximise financial security. A keynote speech should create a need to listen and learn. A humorous after dinner speech should reinforce camaraderie and leave the participants in a positive state of mind.

Focus on *your* desired outcome. What will be different – and better – because of your speech? This is critical. Simplify it to one sentence: 'If they leave with this (skill, ability, technique, attitude, awareness), my objective will have been achieved'. If you don't leave the audience better off than it was before you got there, then there is no point in having been there at all.

ANALYSING THE AUDIENCE

A great deal has been said and written elsewhere about the importance of analysing an audience. True, analysis is important; but not to discover what an audience *wants*, but rather to help you decide how best to get across what it *needs*. The first step, then, is to decide precisely what outcome you are seeking. The second step, audience analysis, reverses the point of view, focusing on what is likely to move your audience to do what you want them to do.

> **Desired outcome remains paramount.**

Audience orientation creates a willingness to listen to messages designed to achieve this outcome.

Doing your homework

Here are five helpful ways you can find out about the composition, knowledge and expectations of an audience:

- Think carefully about what you already know about this particular audience and situation.

- Consult with other individuals or groups who have addressed the same audience.

- Review examples of the work of your audience.

- Debrief after each session and assess the audience's reactions.

- Either speak directly with selected audience members or form your impressions indirectly by consulting with their colleagues.

Being audience-oriented

If you include the last option as part of your audience analysis, do so well ahead of time. So as not to take too much of either their time or your own, tell them that you simply want to ask them three quick questions to better prepare your remarks. Ask anything you like to gain relevant input to your speech. Here are three possibilities:

- What advice would you give to a new person in your position?

- If you could change just one thing at (name of organisation), what would that be?

- What's the biggest challenge you are facing in your job?

Use the results to help pitch the speech at the right level, and bring in specific comments and observations at various junctures: 'From what you've told me...'; 'Those of you I've spoken to recently seem to think...'. You can also incorporate this feedback in visual aids, if desired.

Even if you cannot find out much about an audience, try to imagine what they are like. It is better than trying to address rows of empty faces. A speech which is perceived as audience-oriented will always go down better than one that is introspective.

RELATING DESIRED OUTCOME TO AUDIENCE

The desired outcome is known and the nature of the audience established. The crucial question now arises: How can I best act as a catalyst to achieve *this* outcome with *this* audience? The answer is to be *outcome-centred* in your *results focus* and *audience-centred* in your *delivery*. Confuse these at your own peril. Tell them what you need to in order to achieve the desired outcome, but tell them this in a way that makes them feel at ease. It is vital to make your speech as relevant and comfortable for the audience's frame of reference as possible.

> **Comfort is the key to assimilation and acceptance.**

You will not motivate, inform, persuade or entertain if an audience feels uncomfortable. External surroundings are important, but the way people feel *internally* is critical. If they are uncomfortable, they will resist, be diverted and be introspective. If they feel relaxed, unthreatened and 'at home' they will be receptive, open and focused. You can help put *any* audience at ease, and thereby make them more receptive to your message, by doing four things:

- projecting your personality
- injecting a little humour into your speech
- recognising there are different learning styles – and reacting to them
- appealing to their needs or emotions.

Projecting your personality
As an audience member, the worse feeling you can have is embarrassment for the person on stage. If the speaker is uncomfortable, the audience will be uncomfortable. When you are sitting in a relaxed situation with friends or colleagues, talking naturally, the chances are that you are listening to what everyone else is saying and they are listening to you. You need to recognise, then capture this normal style of communication, and make it work for you in *any* given situation. If you are comfortable, your audience will feel comfortable.

Injecting a little humour

People are always relaxed by humour, but since most humour is based upon someone else's discomfort, it is often safer to be self-effacing. People will commiserate and empathise ('Been there; done that; got the tee-shirt'). They will identify not merely with your situation, but with your ensuing message.

You do not need to be a stand-up comedian, indeed you should not be. But you must allow the humorous side of your personality to shine through. Some of us are naturally witty, but most of us are not. If you cannot tell jokes, then recall personal anecdotes. They always go down well provided they are used in context and the point of the story is obvious. They will create that all-important ingredient: instant comfort. Build humour into *every* speech you make.

Recognising there are different learning styles

The best speech preparation embraces the philosophy that people are diverse and learn in varying manners. This has a number of implications for the speaker, and his preparation and attitude:

- Provide for varied sources of input. For example, use audio-visual aids as well as script, have handouts as well as slides.

- Never demand participation in any activity that even one person could find demeaning and uncomfortable. Ask for volunteers.

- Do not take things personally. Embrace every question as honest and sincere, unless you have incontrovertible evidence to the contrary.

- Treat your audience with respect. Do not include stories or exercises simply to make yourself look good. Your content should support your message, and your message should help you achieve your desired outcome.

Appealing to their needs or emotions

Every successful speaker appeals to one or more *needs* or *emotions*. You want them to feel comfortable, to feel unthreatened, to feel there is something in it for them. When you talk to an audience, or perhaps to a key individual within that group, whom you have assessed as dominant and powerful, appeal to their *ego needs* (the ability to influence others). When you talk to an audience of more submissive, dependent types, appeal to their *social needs* (the need to be accepted).

Under the right circumstances (your desired outcome and audience), each of the following appeals can be useful.

Power
By doing what you suggest, your listeners will increase their power or influence:

> '. . . and that would mean your department would assume overall responsibility for the whole process.'

Pride
This is an appeal to honour and self-respect:

> 'We've been the number one for a decade. Surely we are not going to give it up – at least not without one almighty fight.'

Courage
Stand up and be counted:

> 'It's going to be a very difficult few months, but we must face the challenge head-on.'

Desire
This is a basic appeal to self-interest:

> 'If we complete the order by next week, we'll all get that bonus payment.'

Convention
We are all, to varying degrees, creatures of habit. This appeal is intended to make them feel safe by providing examples of where the desired outcome has been successfully achieved elsewhere:

> '. . . and when the County Golf Club increased their fees, their membership actually went up.'

Posterity
They will not be forgotten:

> '. . . and, with your permission, we will name the building Bloggs House.'

Sociability
This appeal works with people who need to be liked:

> '. . . as well as that, your staff will be under far less pressure, and I'm sure they will thank you for that.'

Reputation
If you give a person a good reputation, he will tend to live up to it:

'I'm sure you can do it . . you've never missed a deadline yet.'

Intellect
When talking to a highly rational person (or one who believes himself to be), use logical and intellectual arguments:

'. . . QED.'

Sentiment
Appeals to sentiment, benevolence, or pity can be very effective if you want to appeal on behalf of a charity. But they are rarely effective at work:

'Skip a meal and save a life.'

REMAINING ON-MESSAGE

In a business speech, facts should be secondary to messages. While you may well have drawn your message from facts, when you make a speech, begin with that message and then support it by relevant facts, not vice versa. Include only enough facts to make the message clear. Put together a speech that focuses on what you want the audience – or perhaps that man sitting in the front row – to know, think, or do. Then select enough facts – the right facts – to support that knowledge, thought or action.

Boil your message down to one sentence. Put it on a yellow sticky note, and attach it to your computer monitor or desk. In this way you can look at it periodically and make sure you are still on track. Everything you say, do or show should support this message. Always keep it in mind.

Always remain on-message.

If you do not know what message you intend to convey each time you speak, neither will your audience. Just 'to tell them a new sales campaign will be initiated next month' is not even a message, it is a fact. Nor does it relate directly to the needs of the audience. Unless you want people to fidget, fall asleep or walk out, you must have something to say that the audience will want to hear. You may care passionately about the new campaign, but your audience won't care less if they don't feel it's relevant to them. The essence of a good message is that it will trigger an *emotional response*. You need to find out what they really care about and what their needs are. You need to sell benefits, not features: 'Here's how we plan to reward and support your efforts!'

Knowing what the audience will be asking

From the moment you begin your speech, members of the audience will be asking themselves three things:

- Is this message for me?
- Can I believe this message?
- Is the speaker on my side?

Let's consider what you, the speaker, must do and say to make sure they come up with the right answers.

Is this message for me?
Of course, the audience cannot answer this rationally until they have heard the whole of your message. But people are not rational. They will be asking the question from the moment you first open your mouth – in fact, probably from a lot earlier. This gives you a wonderful opportunity to get in quickly with the right answer. You should tell the audience quite clearly: Yes, this message *is* for you.

'You can become a millionaire without even buying a lottery ticket!'

Your audience will *identify* with such a message and will sit up and pay attention.

Can I believe this message?
People like messages they can check against what they already know, or believe or feel. Before you try to influence your audience, win their trust. Give them a piece of information they already have; suggest an option they already hold; express an emotion they already feel. If your first statement matches with their own knowledge, opinion or feelings, they will approve of it – and of you. Contrary to popular opinion, people will *not* object to being told something they already know. They find it reassuring. More importantly, it enhances your credibility.

An experienced speaker often goes one step further: he admits to one fact which obviously mitigates against his argument. Again, it will be a fact which is already familiar to the audience, or which they can easily deduce for themselves:

> 'As you are aware from our experience at Norwich, a project like this does have an element of risk.'

In this way the speaker earns himself a nod of agreement and achieves a number of plus points. This single, apparently throw-away line has:

* told them something they already know
* acknowledged how clever the audience is
* shown the speaker to be honest, astute and objective
* stolen the thunder of any objectors.

Is the speaker on my side?
Internal audiences like a speaker who is one of them, or at least someone who sees things from their point of view. So identify yourself with them. Talk about *our* competitors; the problems *we* face; the best way for *us* to go forward. External audiences will feel patronised if you talk in this way because clearly you are *not* one of them. Instead use language which shifts the focus away from you and on to them. They are the important people. Talk about *your* competitors; the problems *you* face; the best way for *you* to go forward.

Using the right language

Whatever the nature of the audience, always express yourself in simple terms, and show that you don't intend to bamboozle them with fancy words or complex logic. If possible, use a little of the audience's phraseology or language – but not its jargon – to express a perception special to that audience. Jimmy Carter endeared himself to the people of Newcastle when he declared 'Ha' way the lads!' and John F. Kennedy used the same technique memorably at the height of the Cold War, when he announced to his West German audience: 'Ich bin ein Berliner'.

PUTTING THE RIGHT SLANT ON IT

You always need a context – a message slant or angle, a tone and length appropriate to the specific topic and specific audience. The way you fine-tune and handle your message makes the crucial difference in the audience's acceptance or rejection. Clearly the message slant at a fundraising event would be different from that at a shareholders' meeting. The tone at a church eulogy would be different from that at an employee retirement party. Remarks introducing a guest speaker would be briefer than a detailed motivational talk. What is perhaps less obvious is that there should be differences in message slant, tone and timing of speeches conveying essentially the same information, but to different audiences with different desired outcomes in mind.

Sales volume has been ten per cent below projection for the last three months. This needs to be conveyed to the board, marketing managers and sales force. The information is the same but the slant different:

Audience: Board of Directors
Desired outcome: They are aware of the situation
Message: Don't panic
Angle: We should have foreseen this: new competitor; reorganisation of marketing territory. Our projection was unrealistic
Tone: Informational
Timing: 4–5 minutes.

Audience: Marketing managers
Desired outcome: A new strategy that will generate a ten per cent increase in demand
Message: We need to improve
Angle: We must increase demand for our product, despite the unfavourable market conditions
Tone: Cautious warning
Timing: 15–20 minutes.

Audience: Salespeople
Desired outcome: Sales volume increased by ten per cent
Message: You can do it!
Angle: You have already proved you are the best. We are going to give you all the help we can to fight the new competition and increase market awareness of our product
Tone: Motivational
Timing: 30–40 minutes.

QUESTIONS AND ANSWERS

I've heard it said that a speaker can be speaker-centred, audience-centred or outcome-centred. What does this mean and which style is best?

By definition, a speaker-centred speaker is a self-centred speaker. He seeks personal feedback and gratification, preferably in the form of a standing ovation. At best he projects an interesting persona; at worst he is an egomaniac. Audience-centred speakers are more effective. They give the audience what it wants. They are usually popular public speakers, and sometimes that's good enough.

Outcome-centred speakers do not necessarily give an audience what it wants; they give it what it needs. An effective outcome-centred speaker prepares and presents an audience-oriented script in order to ensure a receptive hearing. However, the bottom line is to achieve the desired outcome. The best style? Outcome-centred. They are the true professionals.

What are the most common mistakes made by corporate speech-makers?

Three themes recur in the business environment, even when organisations have spent considerable time, effort and money in communicating systems:

– Information is confused with communication. Speeches tend to contain far too many facts and figures. This does not generate understanding. In many cases such information overload does the opposite.

– The content is not relevant to the audience. The nature of the information is too technical, too business-jargon loaded or geared to the wrong audience. The information you would give to your shareholders may not necessarily be the information your employees need to know.

– Speeches do not open up opportunities for sharing and pooling. They should facilitate challenge, question assumptions made and generate a true understanding about what the other person, team or manager is trying to say; and they should be about the ability to shape and influence those views as well. The feedback does not have to be immediate, but the audience should be invited to reflect on what has been said and given the opportunity to react and respond. Remember that the word *communication* comes from the Latin *communicare*, which means *to share*.

Is professional speaking a branch of showbusiness?

Whenever you address an audience you step onto a stage, metaphorically and possibly literally. To that extent it is a branch of showbiz. But speakers, like audiences, are diverse. There is a spectrum of speaking that ranges from the totally choreographed to totally *ad hoc* and responsive. Both extremes are occasionally appropriate but more often than not a successful professional speaker, like a successful professional entertainer, will be somewhere in the middle. The best speakers create a speech structure but also carry plenty of spare examples, anecdotes and illustrations in their heads. They know instinctively what will interest *this* audience at *this* time, and what will not. They project their own innate personality. They rely on their natural powers of communication. They rehearse and familiarise themselves with their material, but they do not put on an act.

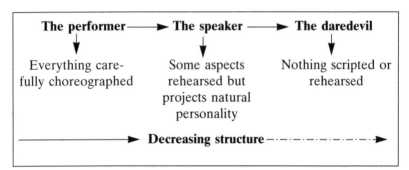

Fig. 1. Professional speaking: a continuum.

CASE STUDIES

Michael doesn't consider the outcome

Michael is an IT manager. The chairman asks him to speak to accounts about the new software package that will be introduced next month. Michael does not attempt to find out the intended outcome of this presentation (it is to ensure that they understand and can use the updated creditor file). Rather he sees his job as simply presenting technical information about the software without any regard as to how this will improve the audience's condition. This is the equivalent of a salesperson making sales calls and considering the job well done. A speech is a means to an end, not an end in itself. Salespeople should bring in new business; speakers should improve the condition of an audience by achieving planned outcomes.

Linda times it well

Linda is the closing speaker at a conference on energy conservation. She waits patiently in the wings while the spokesperson for a conservation pressure group uses up all of his time and a quarter of hers, with the chairman looking on impassively. She cuts down her speech and the conference finishes on time. Linda appreciates that no audience or event organiser ever complains if a wonderful speech runs ten minutes short, but once you overrun by just one minute (individually or collectively), you begin to lose large segments of the audience's attention and goodwill.

Jim makes his audience feel uncomfortable

Five minutes into a seminar on interpersonal skills, Jim asks each participant to tell their neighbour about the most embarrassing moment of their life. One woman turns to the person to her left, and says: 'This is'. Jim's inappropriate request leaves many of his audience feeling upset, unhappy and uncomfortable – and unable or unwilling to learn.

SUMMARY

- Be outcome-centred in your results focus.

- Be audience-centred in your delivery.

- Make your audience feel comfortable.

- Have a simple, believable message that is tailor-made for your audience.

- Remain on-message.

- Give your speeches the right slant.

3
Creating a Speech

The body of any specific address must express in essence what *you* know and feel and trust is right to achieve *your* intended outcome. The message that you impart has to be yours. Yet the way you convey it, the way you structure your speech, can be analysed and perfected. Organisation is the key to clarity. There are five rules to remember when creating a successful speech:

- base the speech on messages, not facts
- jump-start your subconscious creativity
- mind-map the speech
- think like a listener
- write like a talker.

TAKING A MESSAGE-BASED APPROACH

There is no universal, unchanging way to structure a speech. Formats vary according to several determining factors such as different objectives, audiences, surroundings and speakers. However, one general *approach* to speech creation always works, regardless of chosen structure: focusing on messages, not facts.

> **Part of the challenge of creating an effective speech is not so much knowing what to include – but knowing what to leave out.**

It is particularly difficult to eliminate facts when you know how important they have been in forming your opinions. It is all too easy to conclude that the listeners must also know every fact or they won't believe what you are saying. This is *not* the case. A **message-based** approach makes facts secondary. Listeners need to be given only those facts which support your *message*. The facts prove that this message is sound.

Your message may have been influenced by your knowledge,

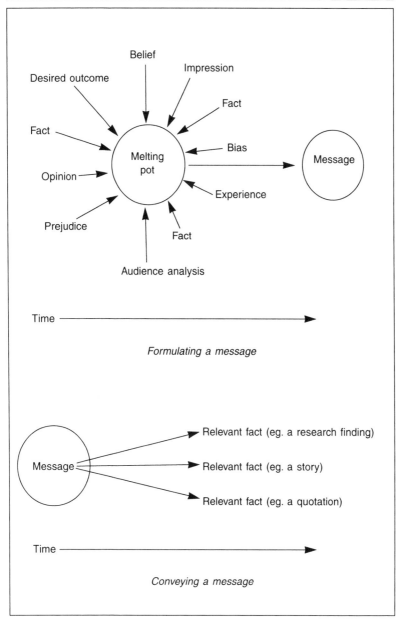

Fig. 2. Formulating a message and conveying it.

opinions and life experiences. It certainly should have been influenced by your audience analysis and the desired outcome. When you convey this message to an audience you should not attempt to describe or justify the way you came to formulate the message. Rather simply select the most persuasive facts to support it.

Generally three relevant facts are enough to support any message or sub-message; often one key fact is adequate. If your message is: 'I am innocent of this crime' and you have the cast-iron alibi that you were at Buckingham Palace, being awarded an OBE, at the time the offence was committed, there is no point in then continuing to argue that you could not possibly have been the perpetrator because you are left-handed or because you have a fear of spiders.

Identifying the context, message, route map and intended outcome

In order for a message-based approach to be effective, you must be clear about the context, message, road map and intended outcome of the speech:

- *The context.* Why are you making this speech? What situation exists, or has occurred, or is likely to occur that brings you and your audience together?

- *The message.* What thought or image do you wish to implant?

- *The route map.* What facts must you discuss so that the audience can have confidence in the veracity of your message and any sub-messages?

- *The intended outcome.* What must the audience know, think or do when you have completed your speech?

The context

It is essential that you bring the audience together. Why are they here today? The way to do this is to outline the *present* situation. Everyone should start with the same basic knowledge. By showing that you understand their situation you will gain their confidence and you will be granted a further hearing. You must establish common ground. It may only take a couple of sentences or it may need quite a long analysis of how things came to be the way they are. But some statement of the current situation has to be made and *agreed upon.*

There must be some significant change, danger, worry or opportunity, or you would not be making this speech. Your success often depends on discovering or implanting some unease, guilt or fear in the person or persons you are trying to win over. For example, you could tell them about business rivals who are now producing improved goods more efficiently. Nobody is interested in salvation until they have experienced a fear of damnation.

The message
Your message must be at the heart of the speech. Have one clear, simple message and then remain on-message throughout. Try to anticipate your audience's evaluation of that message. Imagine how you would react. What questions would you ask? Then articulate probable queries and doubts in the form of rhetorical questions:

'How many of our big customers – Category A here – do you suppose were down in Category D three years ago?'

When you have posed such a question, give your audience time to think about the answer. You need not wait for them to answer; often you can answer it yourself or say:

'I hope that has set you thinking. Now let's move on to our next point.'

The route map
Take the audience into your confidence. Tell them where you will be taking them and how long the journey will take. Your message and sub-messages must be supported by facts. Think carefully about the number of sub-messages and facts you intend to present. Many speakers are far too ambitious in the range of ideas they attempt to cover. Cut it down to no more than three or four.

Your facts should provide rationale, defence, statistical proof, expert quotes or advice, or anything else you find to uphold your assertions. It is more important to have quick, defensible proof than to over-explain every last detail. If necessary, this can be done by means of handouts or at question and answer time. Don't worry about telling them things you think they already know. Unless you do so in a patronising manner, they will find this perfectly acceptable and they may well nod in agreement. And it is quite possible they did *not* know this before you told them, however obvious it may have seemed to you.

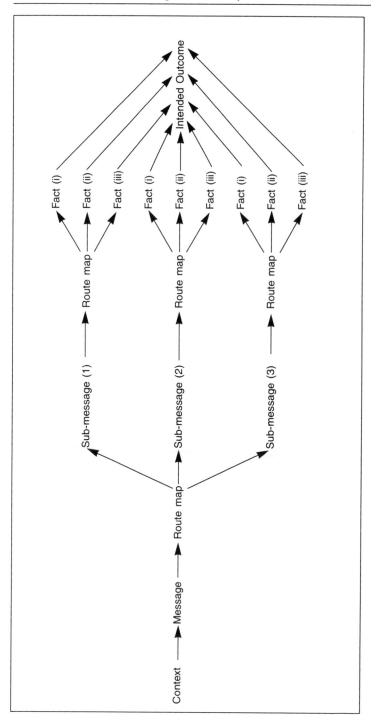

Fig. 3. A message-based approach to speechmaking.

Never overestimate an audience's knowledge and never underestimate its intelligence.

The intended outcome
Outcome is all. There is nothing wrong with getting people fired up briefly, but the vital medium- and long-term benefit you must bring is to improve the audience's condition by providing the required skills, techniques and approaches that people continue to demonstrate every day long after you have spoken.

JUMP-STARTING YOUR SUBCONSCIOUS CREATIVITY

Visualise a person being creative. Put the book down for a few moments and imagine someone actually *creating* something. What did you see? The odds are that you saw an inventor, a painter, a musician, a scientist, or some other specialist producing an important new product, a piece of art or a scientific finding. Of course all these people were being creative, but the view that creativity must involve great achievements is far too narrow. Why did you not see an *ordinary* person – perhaps yourself – making something or solving some problem – or creating a speech? As the American psychologist, Abraham Maslow put it: 'A first-rate soup is more creative than a second-rate painting.'

Creativity is *not* confined to the gifted few; creative people are not a race apart. Nor are they necessarily particularly clever. Albert Einstein had to spend an extra year in high school before being accepted by the Zurich Polytechnic School, and when he left they would not recommend him for a job; F. Scott Fitzgerald may have penned *The Great Gatsby*, but he was anything but a great speller; and Charles Darwin would not have survived even the most basic test of numeracy.

Getting great ideas
You rarely arrive at a very big idea solely through a conscious, rational thought process. It usually comes from the subconscious mind. The essence of creativity is to be able to look at familiar objects and situations, enriched by experience but not constrained by it. Or, in the words of Arthur Koestler: 'The creative art consists in combining previously unrelated structures in such a way that you get more out of the emergent whole than you have put in.' He was describing a creative synergy where 2 plus 2 make 5.

Stages in the creative process

Accounts gathered first hand suggest there are usually four stages in the creative process:

- Preparation: knowing precisely what you want to achieve.

- Incubation: letting this sink into the subconscious mind and allowing the mind to work on it.

- Illumination: Eureka!

- Verification: putting the solution to the test.

Preparation

It is essential to know precisely what you want to achieve. Serendipity has to be earned. It is no substitute for a detailed knowledge of your subject. It is a bonus to it. Or, to quote Louis Pasteur: 'Chance favours the prepared mind'. If the desired outcome is defined too narrowly it will inhibit creative solutions. As a general rule, the more broadly an objective can be stated, the more room becomes available for conceptualisation. However, never define the desired outcome so broadly that it becomes meaningless.

Convert **content skills** into **process skills**. Don't think in terms of the motor car industry, insurance or electronics. Think in terms of decision-making, negotiating or problem solving. If your mind is set on a wider focus, it will observe or take in what others would eliminate as irrelevant or accidental. Your subconscious mind cannot get to work on a problem until it knows what it *is* – and possibly what it is *not*.

Incubation

Next comes the incubation stage and there are a number of techniques you can apply to help it on its way. However, paradoxically, you must not try too hard. Be aware of what is possible and then relax and just let it happen. You have got used to relying on your rational faculties which are associated with the left side of the brain and you tend to ignore the bizarre and unconventional thoughts that arise from the emotional and imaginative right side of the brain. However, these thoughts are just as valuable since they give us our most creative insights and our most inventive solutions to problems.

Ideas are constantly swimming about in the brain searching like sperms for the egg they can join to produce a new idea. The brain is full of lonely ideas begging you to make some sense of them, to recognise them as interesting. The lazy brain just files them away in old pigeon holes like a bureaucrat who wants an easy life. The lively brain picks and chooses and creates new insights out of ideas.

Allow your subconscious mind to take over; let your critical facility relax. Sleep on it. Make a note of *all* your thoughts. The relevance of some of them may not become apparent for hours, or days, or weeks. They may connect with subsequent thoughts, as an apparently insignificant detail assumes great importance and an apparently important one takes a back seat. Ideas happen when thoughts collide. Encourage collision.

Illumination
Scientists frequently affirm that their moments of insight happened away from the laboratory. William Harvey was repairing a water pump when he made the unexpected connection between the pump and the human heart and he went on to develop the modern theory of blood circulation. Orville Wright was cycling in the countryside when he first made the connection between a bicycle, a bird's wing and an engine. Creative ideas are break-through ideas. They pierce the barriers of habit, cliché, patterns and conformity. In short, they allow us to see the world – or at least a part of it – in new, exciting and imaginative ways. But all such apparent insights must, of course, be rigorously tested.

Verification
The peculiarity of humans is that we can watch ourselves as we go about our business, as we talk and think. We have, as it were, two internal voices so we can both create new ideas and look at them, criticise or admire. It is time for reason and logic to leave the substitute's bench. The conscious brain takes over and evaluates the suggestions it has been given by its subconscious counterpart. At this stage, many apparent insights are proved to be flawed – but others are verified. Yes, Friedrich Kekule's dream of the structure of benzine was correct. Yes, Neils Bohr's bath-time visualisation of the model of atomic structure was accurate.

Being open-minded
During your schooldays you were led to believe that most questions can be solved by one – and *only one* – correct solution (7 x 8 = ?). As you grew up you discovered that things are rarely so straightforward. There is often more than one right answer, and sometimes there are no wrong answers. Yet your early encounters of an

apparently simple world of black and white, of right and wrong, may well have resulted in you developing a one-right-answer approach to problems in life generally. This is an anathema to creative thinking which requires the ability to come up with *many* ideas and *many* possible solutions.

As you prepare your speech, do not immediately accept the first or most obvious message, thought or fact that comes to you. Look for alternatives.

Do not set too high a standard in the early stages, and do not reject anything too quickly. Make it a habit to search for a little longer and to dig just a little deeper. The subconscious is shy, elusive and unwieldy, but it *is* possible to learn to tap it and even direct it.

A bunch of bananas
The next time you are facing a difficult problem, throw in a bunch of bananas. Open a dictionary randomly, turn away and point at a word – perhaps *banana*. This work will release you from your current dominant – and possibly unimaginative – mind-set. Say an advertising executive is considering how to make cigarette tips more acceptable to the public. He throws in the word *stem*. Why not put a seed in each tip so discarded ends produce flowers?

The knight's move
Schizophrenics sometimes make statements without any apparent reason behind them. For years doctors considered this totally illogical; but later it was realised that the thinking was logical but several steps had been omitted in the logic. This was dubbed the knight's move, an allusion to way a knight jumps over pieces in a *non-linear* fashion in chess. This is often associated with creative thinking. When your mind jumps from A to D, instead of going through the usual ABCD, try to work out what the missing sequence might have been. The more you recognise that moves have occurred, and the more you successfully interpret them, the more your subconscious mind will make these creative moves.

Lateral thinking
If our ideas are only a summary of what we already know, how can we get new ideas? We need some jolting or provoking system. One such system is Edward de Bono's now famous lateral thinking. There's nothing mystical or magical about it; it merely involves look-

ing at things from all angles, not merely head-on. Lateral thinking may not always produce a solution or a new idea, but it will almost always provide a new starting point from which solutions can be sought, perhaps through logical thinking.

A brain of two halves

Much research has gone into the workings of the human brain. An over-simplistic, yet useful model of the brain is one of a cortex divided into halves, or hemispheres, each being good at different things.

You must learn how to turn off your left-mode thinking, and turn on your right-mode thinking. One deceptively simple way to do this is to think about a problem while you are engaged in some physical activity, such as jogging, or while you are feeling very relaxed (perhaps in the bath, in the local, or immediately before or after sleep). Another method is to give your brain a task which the left hemisphere *cannot* – or *will not* – handle, such as making sense of abstract lines and shapes. It will reject the task and the imaginative right hemisphere will accept the challenge instead.

It is easy to recognise when you are engaged in right-mode thinking. Time will seem to fly by. You will be almost unaware of what would normally be considered distractions. You will be active yet very calm. You will be thinking in images, not words. You will be engrossed in the task. Creative ideas do not come to the half-hearted. The stereotype of the absent-minded professor, so absorbed in his thoughts that he fumbles through the routine tasks of everyday life, is an amusing yet essentially accurate picture of right-mode thinking in action.

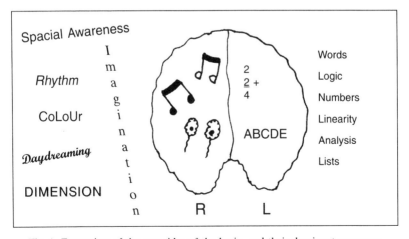

Fig. 4. Front view of the two sides of the brain, and their dominant processes.

MIND MAPPING A SPEECH

Mind Mapping® is a technique originated by Tony Buzan. The theory is that the brain does not work as well in a linear or list-like format because the brain acts on triggers which stimulate new thoughts – it thinks laterally rather than vertically so although a complete brain pattern may appear untidy to you, to your brain it is clear and logical.

Rather than starting notes at the *top* of a page and working down in sentences or lists, you start at the *centre* with your message and branch out as dictated by sub-messages and associated ideas and evidence. You have three concentric circles. The smallest circle contains your central message; the middle-sized circle contains your sub-messages; and the largest circle contains your supporting facts.

A mind mapped speech has a number of advantages over the traditional linear form of drafting:

- The central message (literally) is more clearly defined.

- The facts which support each sub-message are clearly identified.

- Unnecessary facts will not be included.

- The links between the key concepts, sub-messages and supporting facts will immediately be recognisable because of the proximity and connection.

- The nature of the structure allows for easy addition of new information.

- The open-ended nature of the map will enable the brain to make new connections far more readily. Expect to be surprised.

Figure 5, on page 47, shows a possible mind map for an informal ten-minute speech to employees. The desired outcome of the speech is: 'Our image will be improved and we will achieve a 90 per cent-plus approval rating within a year.' Its central message is: 'The more people know us, the better they like us.'

A mind map is *spacial*. It has, as yet, no time sequence. The central message may represent the beginning of the speech. More likely, though, it will represent the main body of the speech. At this stage what matters is that a total argument is seen to emerge. How far does the complete picture radiate naturally from the central message? If a thought or fact or sub-message does not radiate, it will be difficult to make the speech coherent and interesting. More importantly, it will not support your central message, so it has no place in the speech.

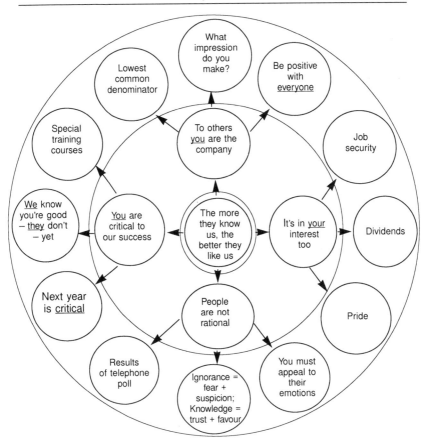

Fig. 5. Mind mapping a speech.

Converting spacial to temporal structure

Creating a coherent design is the first step in ensuring the audience receive what you intend them to. The next step is to transform the spacial design into a *time sequence*. You must re-shape your material to assist reception of your argument. You must be able to take your audience with you every step of the way. The argument must develop from the known to the unknown. It has to lead logically to your conclusion. Each step must be related to the previous step and by the time the conclusion is reached the inevitability of the route of the argument must be accepted.

A good method of temporal structure development is to transcribe each sub-message on an index card, with key words relating to the two or three supporting facts below each of them. You will then find it easy to add new cards, remove others and rearrange them until you have achieved your optimal framework: chronological, geographical, problem solving order or some other arrangement. Think like a listener. Write like a talker.

THINKING LIKE A LISTENER

It is essential to gain and maintain interest. And what everyone is interested in above everything else is himself. Continually ask yourself: Why should he be interested in this message? Why should he feel or think or do what I want him to? What's in it for him? If you think like a listener you will enlist his cooperation better.

You need to think about the kinds of thing that will have a positive effect on your audience and stick in their memories. Written information should be *easy to find*. Spoken and visual communication should be *easy to remember*.

Showing pictures

People remember things much more easily if they are connected to *right brain* stimulation. The way to stimulate the right brain is to show pictures. People remember visual stimuli. Can you recall the title and subtitle of this book? Yet I am sure you can remember the colour of the cover.

Most of what is shown during business speeches and presentations is a waste of effort – at best. If a visual aid does not help the audience understand and remember the point you are making then replace it or leave it out. It is far better to first decide your message and sub-messages and then how to best support them, rather than deciding what use you can make of the media you may have access to. Make sure they see everything you want them to remember.

Good visual aids are:

- clear
- simple
- original
- easy to see
- easy to grasp
- stimulating
- creative
- reinforcing your message or submessage.

Using presentations software
If you follow the guidelines that come with the package, your so-

called visual aids will contain more verbal than visual information. If you insist on putting up screens full of words, then keep it simple. Remember the tee-shirt test: never use more words on a screen than you would on a tee-shirt.

- Use only two different fonts, in two different point sizes.

- Don't highlight too much through *italics*, CAPITALS or **bold**. The more things you emphasise, the less powerful each emphasis becomes.

- Don't use fancy borders which are more interesting than the words inside them.

- Try to find ways of using the software creatively, to produce fresh-looking and original visual aids.

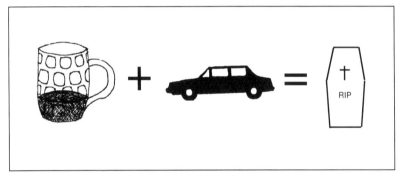

Fig. 6. Making a visual aid unique and memorable.

Using analogy

A well chosen parallel from within the audience's experience can save ten minutes of involved explanation. It does not need to be comprehensive, just clear, brief and relevant. This one would work well for an audience of advertising executives.

'Any advertisement has to be judged on four criteria:

- *Visibility*. What does it stand for?

- *Identity*. Is the brand name registered?

- *Promise*. What is the benefit for the potential customer?

- *Single-mindedness*. Is everything in the advert pointed the same way and helping to put across the promise to the recipient?

It is the same with a speech. You must test your script against the same criteria:

- *Visibility*. Does it stand out (and for the right reasons)?
- *Identity*. Is your name and that of your organisation, company or department firmly locked into the message?
- *Promise*. What's in it for your listeners?
- *Single-mindedness*. Is everything in the script on-message?'

Telling stories

Everyone loves a story. If you can engage your audience with a relevant anecdote you are on to a winner. You will not only grab and hold their attention but also bring your speech to life by evoking strong images in the minds of listeners. You are in practical territory here. If you find a story about Florence Nightingale that would illustrate your message, make a few embellishments here and there and allow your chairman to take the role of the Lady of the Lamp. The key is the audience's improved condition, not historical accuracy. Use anything that works for you.

Keeping the audience in the picture

Matching your choice of anecdotes to the nature of the audience is easy when the group is homogeneous – medical stories for doctors, religious anecdotes for the clergy, horsey tales for the gymkhana club. Help them feel like a special group. Reinforce group identity, perhaps by referring to something or someone you know irritates them:

> 'I hear they are going to erect a huge statue of (the name of their least favourite politician) in Trafalgar Square. They are going to do it so the pigeons can express the views of you all.'

Keep their particular group attitude in mind and find ways to personalise even the most remote issue so they can see the connection between themselves and it. If people can see what you're telling them applies to their lives, they remain interested.

Giving the story a clear moral

Your story should have a point to it, it should support at least one of your sub-messages. Present the sub-message, tell the story, and then reinforce the sub-message. This is a variation of the classic formula: Tell them what you are going to tell them, tell them, and then tell them what you have told them. The way a speaker flows naturally into and out of a story takes a little thought, but it's so worthwhile in its effect:

Sub-message: 'Good product service is never enough.

Supporting story: You may have seen this advertisement used by a training consulting firm: Two colleagues are talking about a particular company and one says, "Their product is fine, but their customer service is a joke." The second person responds, "Oh, well then, who would you recommend?"

Reinforced sub-message: The implication? Customer service is what people are buying.'

Using emotion to good effect

C.S. Forester reminds us that 'Words spoken from the full heart carry more weight than all the artifices of rhetoric.' But emotion in a business speech? Surely it is unprofessional to bring emotion into a business. While there may be no room for passion when your purpose is to inform, you should feel free to display strong personal feelings when you are attempting to persuade people. Expert communicators know that, under the right circumstances, they can gain power by reintroducing emotion into the workplace. However, you *must* be genuine. False heartiness, cheap sincerity and – worst of all – crocodile tears will all be obvious to an audience.

Varying the texture

No two audiences are the same and no two individuals within an audience are the same. Some people rejoice in group learning, others prefer solitary absorption. Some get most from a question and answer session, others benefit most from practical demonstrations. Listening to one person for any length of time can become boring – and the worst thing any speaker can do is to become boring. Ask yourself such questions as:

- Is there too much solid talk at any point?
- Will they be punch drunk with the slide sequence?
- Is there adequate opportunity for feedback?

Keep them interested by being a little unpredictable and by varying the texture of your speech.

Honouring short attention spans

Psychologists have plotted how the attention of an audience varies throughout a presentation. As illustrated in Figure 7, during a 40-minute speech attention starts high, drops gradually for about ten minutes, then more steeply until it reaches its lowest point after about 30 minutes. Then it starts to rise steeply and remains high again for the last five minutes.

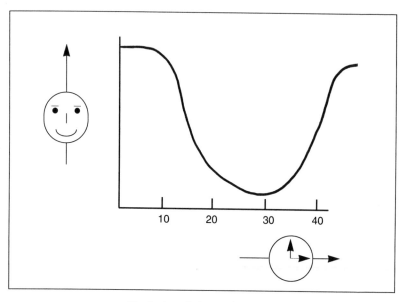

Fig. 7. A typical attention curve.

There are some important lessons to be learnt from this:

- The principle of **primacy and recency** tells us that your most important points must be at the beginning and the end. In particular the last picture and last sentence or phrase will stay in the mind before new images and words are piled on top of them.

- It is important to build in plenty of texture variations after the first ten minutes, devices to revive and maintain attention.

- The audience's attention will not rise towards the end of a session unless they know the end is in sight.

How many times have you been sorry that a presentation has reached a break? Now think how many times you have been glad. Enough said? Breaks are high points and most presentations have too few. It is far better to have three ten-minute breaks than one half-hour break.

WRITING LIKE A TALKER

Spoken words are different from written words: the first are structured in time; the second are structured in space. Putting across an argument in a purely spoken form demands that both the speaker and the listener are *always* at the same place in the argument. Simultaneous comprehension is essential. There can be no replays. Breaking up the thought into separate elements, into a sequence of short, simple, one-thought sentences, is one way of ensuring this.

A degree of repetition is essential in spoken communication.

Important ideas, facts and opinions need to be continually reinforced to ensure the listener keeps up with the speaker.

This is known as **redundancy** as no new information is provided. Once again, the objective is simultaneous comprehension. The more your audience knows about the topic, the less redundancy needs to be supplied.

The order of words is different, too. We seem subconsciously to understand the best order when we speak, but we lose the knack when we write a script. The lesson is clear: Speak your words out loud before you commit them to paper. You will find that each element, each phrase, each sentence, will be built from what has gone before. Instinctively, you will take your listeners from the known to the unknown; from the general to the particular; from agreement to disagreement; from present to future.

'Orange believe you shouldn't be rushed into anything. Which is why we offer a 14-day money-back guarantee. The future's bright. The future's Orange.'

This is English written to be read out loud. It includes:

- one simple idea
- short words (average five letters)
- short sentences (average eight words)
- a link (Which is why . . .) ·

- effective repetition (The *future's* bright. The *future's* Orange)
- impact words (guarantee, you)
- primacy and recency (Orange, Orange).

Forget all about the rules of grammar and syntax, relax and write as you talk.

Text	Script
• is a journey at the reader's pace	• is a journey at the presenter's pace
• can be re-read if necessary	• is heard once only
• can be read in any order	• is heard in the order it is presented
• can easily be ignored	• cannot easily be ignored
• cannot convey sincerity	• can convey genuine commitment
• cannot be reinforced or modified	• can be reinforced by body language or modified in response to feedback
• is useful for conveying information	• is useful for conveying messages
• is not memorable.	• can be memorable.

QUESTIONS AND ANSWERS

My speech is too short. How should I expand it?

It is not essential to use all the time allocated to you. An audience will appreciate it if you finish a few minutes early, and an event organiser will have no objections so long as the planned outcome has been, or will be achieved. However, you should not finish *too* early, specially if another speaker follows you. Add examples to support your message or sub-messages. If you are using visual aids, consider a couple of additional supporting ones. For longer presentations, think about more audience involvement.

My speech is too long. Should I drop my anecdotes?

Stories liven up a speech. Drop as few of them as possible. If necessary drop a sub-message instead. It is far better to have just two sub-messages, each supported by a story, than four sub-messages with no supporting stories.

I am going to make a series of speeches abroad. Can you offer any additional advice?

The following suggestions can help you communicate more effectively with people from other countries and cultures:

- Declare your pleasure at speaking to this foreign audience.
- Cite an expert from your guest's country or culture.
- Include a quotation from your guest's country or culture.
- Stress that people share common feelings.
- Deliver your most important line in the audience's language.
- Use the country's measurement terms.
- Reinforce the need for intercultural communication.

CASE STUDIES

Jane comes up with a novel idea

Jane is a research scientist who has been asked to talk about the work that led to the development of a new product. Knowing how useful stories are in a speech, she decides to base the entire presentation on just *one* story – the story of how she came to be making this presentation! 'Two years ago we began the research project...'. She then plots her learning process, message and supporting facts: 'We soon came across the problem of...'; 'The solution proved fascinating...'; 'The next step was to...'; 'Help came from an unexpected source...'. And so on. Her unusual approach proves highly effective.

Duncan wakes them up

Duncan, a charity director, is invited to address a conference on international aid. The event begins disappointingly with a series of speakers merely trotting out endless facts and figures. When Duncan speaks, the conference comes to life. For every point he makes he finds an anecdote, metaphor or analogy which illustrates it and links it to his central message. By doing so he builds mental pictures in the minds of his audience. He makes complex concepts understandable by using examples which are familiar to the audience, whether from the world of work or the everyday world of the family. His words come alive, his personality shines through, he gets his message across – and he achieves his desired outcome.

William thinks on his feet

William is the chairman of a shoe-making company. He wants to find a humorous little anecdote he can use during an after dinner speech about a managing director who never stops urging his sales force to strive harder for bigger rewards and whose wife is reputed to enjoy shopping. He says: 'Our managing director, Martin, once told me that there is only one thing a man can do if he's married to a wife who enjoys spending money, and that is – learn to enjoy earning it.' The joke goes down well. Later, as the gathering disperses, an American visitor makes his way to the top table and buttonholes William. 'Heh, that line you told us you heard from Martin. . . it's a direct quote from Ed Howe.' 'Good Lord,' says William, 'so Martin's a plagiarist.'

SUMMARY

- Base your speech on messages, not facts.
- Jump-start your subconscious creativity.
- Mind-map your speech.
- Convert spacial to temporal patterning.
- Think like a listener.
- Write like a talker.

4
Designing the Bookends

Think of your opening and closing lines as the verbal bookends of your speech. They must be constructed well enough to support and hold everything that comes between them. Your opening words should motivate your audience to *listen* intently, and your closing words should reinforce your message and motivate them to *act* or *react* as the desired outcome requires. Play around with your bookends until you are satisfied that they will have exactly the effect you are seeking.

FINDING A CAPTIVATING OPENING

As they tell their speakers at Shell, if you don't strike oil within two minutes, stop boring. It is *essential* to start well. Allow yourself plenty of time to find an effective opening. Successful communicators often ponder, consciously and subconsciously, for days over their opening words. They know that the first three sentences of their speech set the course for success or failure: a good start points towards plain sailing, a bad one makes you sail against the wind.

A captivating opening is one that:

- creates excitement, curiosity, positive feelings and impact
- convinces the audience that you know your subject and that you are in control of your material
- demonstrates your awareness of your audience's needs, expectations, composition and interests.

Think about the best and worst business speeches you have heard. How did you feel, as a listener, as they began? How did you respond to the speakers? Did the opening make you sit up and pay attention? Or were you annoyed, embarrassed and indignant? Ask yourself why you felt the way you did.

Making the opening appropriate

The opening of a business speech must be appropriate given the intended outcome and the nature of the audience. It should also be in tune with the rest of the speech. If you open with a joke, your audience will expect more of the same to follow. Every speech is different and every audience is different. What sort of initial impression do you want to make? What are you trying to achieve? Make sure your opening is appropriate to your objective. Appropriateness is the key to effectiveness.

USING THE OPENING TO ACHIEVE YOUR OBJECTIVE

Most business speeches have one of three broad objectives:

- to appeal to self-interest
- to make them think
- to give them a jolt.

Below you will find a selection of tried and tested openings – or hooks, as entertainers call them – that will help you achieve each of these objectives. There are also examples of more unconventional techniques which, under the right circumstances, can make a speech memorable. All of the hooks that follow can be adapted and personalised to help you begin on just the right note.

> **Your opening is an opportunity. Grasp it.**

As soon as you have made your audience sit up and listen, take them into your confidence. Set out the main areas that are going to be covered during the speech. Then make a smooth transition to the first point in the body of your speech. Before anyone knows it, they're committed to listening and the process has begun.

Appealing to self-interest

Here are three openings that unashamedly appeal to basic needs or wants:

- initial benefit promise
- Maslow re-visited
- only three points.

Initial benefit promise (IBP)
The IBP is a classic technique for hooking an audience. It stresses maximum gain for minimum effort. Tell them what's in it for them:

> 'In the next ten minutes you will learn three easy, surefire ways to make more money.'

More money! Easy, surefire! You have their undivided attention.

> 'Would you like to add ten quality years to your life? Then think twice before reaching for that saltcellar. I'm John Bowden and I'm going to share with you three secrets that can add those years to your life.'

An offer surely they can't refuse. You have asked a question that is sure to elicit a silent 'yes' from everyone in the room and, as salespeople know, once you get them saying or thinking 'yes', you are well on your way to closing the deal.

Maslow re-visited
You have already found out a good deal about your audience to help you decide whether you should speak and, if so, what you should say and how you should say it. Why not use this research when devising your opening? Abraham Maslow identified various levels of human need. At any given moment an individual will be aiming to satisfy one, and *only one* particular level of need.

The four levels of need that are of interest to the business speaker are as follows:

- **Security needs level:** the need for shelter and job security.

- **Social needs level:** the need to belong, to be with others and to be accepted by them.

- **Esteem/ego needs level:** the need for respect from others.

- **Self-actualisation needs level:** the need to realise potential.

To motivate an audience, you must consider what level of need the listeners are at and offer appropriate rewards and incentives. Have you identified one overriding audience need that dominates all others? If it is a mixed group, what is likely to motivate the main decision maker(s)? For an 18 year-old school leaver eager to rent his own flat, money might be the determining factor in deciding whether or not to respond to your request or challenge (a security need). An older executive with less pressing financial worries might well be motivated by the promise of a more challenging job (a self-actualisation need).

Here are examples of openings appropriate to each of the four levels of audience need:

'You are looking for a purpose to your commitment. So are we. You want to safeguard the future. So do we.'

'It's a great feeling being part of a winning team, isn't it?'

'Today I am proud to announce the result of our Salesperson of the Year competition.'

'During the next month each of us will be pushed to the limit – and beyond it.'

Only three points
Most business speeches are far too long. Audiences are grateful to any speaker who tells them, in the first few sentences, that this speech will contain no more than three important points. Consciously simplify complicated processes. Delight your audience with straightforward concepts. Your efforts will be rewarded.

'There are just three things that count: health, happiness and hope.'

'Innovation consists of only three parts: defining the problem, searching for ideas, and practical implementation.'

'There are only three points to bear in mind when choosing a compelling opening to a speech. One: create excitement, curiosity, positive feelings and impact. Two: convince the audience that you know the subject and that you are in control of your material. Three: demonstrate your awareness of your audience's needs, expectations, composition and interests. That's it, just three points.'

A word of warning: If you use a self-interest opening, you must deliver the goods. Any listener who, at the end of a speech, concludes that you have not kept your part of the bargain will feel cheated. Your credibility will be shattered. If you make a promise, keep it.

Making them think
Such openings immediately involve an audience, turning passive listeners into active participants. They are most appropriate when you

want people to think deeply about a subject. The three techniques considered here are:

- excite, link and involve
- story or quotation
- question or riddle.

Excite, link and involve (ELI)
ELI is a powerful variation of the 'only three points' opening. Your first remark *excites* the audience with something vivid, interesting, off-beat and unexpected. Your second skilfully reinforces this and *links* it to your third. This vital final remark puts everything into context and *involves* your audience in both your opening and what is to follow.

Antony Jay relates this classic ELI opening which he heard given by an African delegate at an international conference on Third World Aid:

'My mother-in-law does not like me because my father ate her father.' *(Excite. Shocked silence followed by riotous laughter.)*

'You laughed just now when I said my father ate another man. Well, it's true, he did.' *(Link.)*

'You all come from countries which have centuries of civilisation and culture behind you. Yet – you will forgive me – you are all still making economic and political mistakes. My country is one generation removed from cannibalism. Is it surprising we make mistakes and we need – oh ladies and gentlemen – we need your help?' *(Involve.)*

What an opening. The audience was putty in his hands. The speaker went on to show why and how they could help – and they did. That speech truly moved them into action.

It is essential that you economise and discipline yourself to only three short remarks. You are seeking a clean, crisp, immediate communion and a direct response. Experiment until you have got your opening spot on: excite, link and involve.

Story or quotation
Some of the finest speechmakers like to open with a story or quotation which illustrates their purpose and, if possible, their point. This opening need not necessarily be funny; it could well grab the atten-

tion in other ways. It may be a story or short quotation of deep human interest. Many speakers hold back its implication or significance until the end of the speech, thus holding attention right through. An anecdote can be an ideal link into the theme of your speech. If chosen carefully, a good opening will illustrate your topic or indicate exactly where you stand on the subject.

'A man writes to Father Christmas: Dear Santa, "I am desperately in need of £100. Please, please help me, I have no one else to turn to." He addresses it to the North Pole and posts it. In a special, kindly, post office department, the letter is opened. The clerks are genuinely moved by this pathetic appeal and – it being the season of goodwill – decide to have a whip-round. They collect £80 and post it back, "with love from Santa's Grotto". The following day a second letter arrives at the post office: "Thank you so much, dear Father Christmas, for answering my letter. But I think I ought to tell you that those buggers in the post office stole £20!" Sometimes even our most magnanimous gestures are not understood or appreciated.'

How would you, as a listener, react to these two openings?

'This morning I intend to illustrate why research scientists sometimes need to be illogical.'

'While daydreaming on a hill one summer day, Albert Einstein imagined he was riding sunbeams to the far extremities of the universe, and upon finding himself returned, illogically, to the surface of the sun, he realised that the universe must indeed be curved and that his previous logical scientific training had been incomplete. The numbers, equations and words he wrapped around this new image gave us the Theory of Relativity – a left and right brain synthesis.'

The first opening is dull and even patronising. The second brings the subject to life. It allows the audience to share Einstein's daydream and creates an image that you can go back to again and again during the course of your speech.

What good stories and anecdotes have in common is that they make an audience think about a subject, often from a perspective they have not considered before. This gem comes from Heinz Goldman:

'Can you remember what happened 15 billion years ago? The Big Bang. Do you know what happened four million years ago? The formation of the Earth. And one and two million years ago? The first human beings began to develop. Five hundred years ago? The Middle Ages. Now imagine the past 15 billion years as a single year. On 1st January there was the Big Bang, the Earth began to form in September, the human race on 31st December and the Middle Ages took place one hour before midnight. Ladies and gentlemen, does it really matter if we delay our expansion until next summer?'

Your audience has come to hear you, but you can still open with an apt quotation from someone else. Your source could well be a member of the audience, if they have made a point likely to generate a smile or link firmly to your topic. But equally it could well be someone famous or eminent in your field.

'Oscar Wilde said there is only one thing in this world worse than being talked about – and that is *not* being talked about. Today we launch a PR campaign that Oscar would have been proud of.'

' "It must be remembered that there is nothing more difficult to plan, more uncertain of success, nor more dangerous to manage than the creation of a new order of things. For the initiator has the enmity of all who would profit by the preservation of the old institutions, and merely lukewarm defenders in those who would gain by new ones." Good afternoon, I'm John Bowden. That was a quotation from *The Prince*, the famous, or perhaps infamous book by the 16th century political theorist, Niccolo Machiavelli, Machiavelli's ideas aren't to everyone's taste, but he certainly knew a thing or two about today's topic: cultural change.'

'As Tarzan said to Jane as he came home exhausted one night: "It's a bloody jungle out there!".'

Question or riddle
You achieve several benefits by asking a rhetorical question at the beginning of your speech: you establish contact with your audience, arouse their interest and you force them to think. A question can evoke memories and create fertile ground for communication by recalling a common experience.

'Do you remember what happened on 19th October, 1987? That was Black Monday, a day forever etched in our collective memory.'

An opening can consist of up to three consecutive rhetorical questions:

> 'Does training matter? Is it not essential to have a highly skilled workforce? Should we not spend a few minutes thinking about this?'

Alternatively, the question can take the form of a riddle:

> 'What grows bigger the more you take from it? I shall tell you: our budget deficit.'

The topic has been announced and the tone set.

> 'Today I am going to talk about the power that can make the weak strong, that made America more powerful than Russia and that makes dogs bark at night.'

This riddle was posed to an audience of salespeople. The speaker was going to talk about the power of *territory*. Anyone on his own ground is more powerful than visitors and this makes the weak man strong in his own house. America is a country with a history and culture dominated by an expansionist ethos ('Go west, young man'). And dogs that bark in the night? Poetic licence really, but dogs do bark to defend their own territory and are more menacing on their own ground against strangers.

A riddle provides an excellent means of illustrating unexpected and interesting associations and connections. It can also be referred to during, and perhaps solved at the end of a speech.

Giving them a jolt

Sometimes you have to shake people up when trying to activate an apathetic audience or when dealing with difficult issues. If you are to command attention, specially in a large gathering, you need to be larger than life. Most openings benefit from a touch of drama. Three of the most effective ones are:

- shocking image
- striking fact
- controversial statement.

Shocking image
Spell out the implications of your message to your audience. Get the focus firmly onto them and away from you. Telling them that the

opposition out there is tough is nothing like as powerful as creating a mental picture of the implications this has for *them*.

> 'Just picture it. . . the people working in the consummate company of the 21st century. They are active, agile and aware. They know how to harness the best of teams, techniques and technologies. They share a vision. They have a new mission for a new millennium. Now. . . picture competing with this company.'

An image such as this packs a real punch. One mental picture is worth a thousand words.

Striking fact

People generally are not impressed or influenced by masses of facts, figures or statistics. Indeed, they often do not even understand them. Highlighting one simple, surprising fact, curiosity or oddity is a far more effective way to bring home a salient point to a complacent audience:

> 'Research shows that if we give a customer cause to complain, they are likely to tell ten other people. If we please them they will only tell one. Not a ratio to forget.'

As always, choose your words carefully. Round your figures and percentages up or down; relate them to what people know and are used to. Don't say twenty per cent, say one person in five, don't say the probability is minuscule, say you have more chance of winning the Lottery.

> 'Producing a good product is no longer enough. Today people expect – deserve – excellent customer care. When someone says to you that pleasing a customer is hard, ask them: "Compared to what?" To having to find new ones? Believe me, it's far harder to get new customers than to take good care of existing ones. Yet, even so, we have lost six out of every ten customers who were on our books five years ago. Enough to fill Wembley Stadium twice over.'

Controversial statement

A provocative statement will focus attention and whet the appetite of your audience in the same way as a headline in a newspaper. Whether they agree or disagree, they are sure to listen:

> 'The only people who are sane enough to be allowed to own guns are the ones who are sane enough not to want them.'

'Your trainers are made by underfed Indian children and marketed by overpaid American sports stars.'

Architect Frank Lloyd Wright used this technique effectively when speaking in Pittsburg:

'This is the ugliest city I've ever seen.'

Pittsburg sat up and paid attention.

Being off the wall

Your aim is to make your opening memorable – and for all the *right* reasons. If you want to stand out from the pack, why not try something a little different? Here are three possibilities:

- joke or one-liner
- topical reference
- silence.

Joke or one-liner

It is unusual to open a business speech with a joke. However a good one, well told, will gain attention, establish empathy, focus the audience's thinking and put them at ease. The joke must be funny, not too well known and relevant to the subject and the occasion. It is most appropriate when you are known by the audience and your aim is to be entertaining or informative. Never tell a joke unless you feel confident and competent to do so. It is safer to open with a one-liner rather than a long joke. If a thirty-second gag flops, you are in trouble. If a one-liner backfires, probably no one will even notice.

Library shelves are weighed down with books containing jokes and amusing stories that can easily be adapted and personalised. One-liners, on the other hand, are thinner on the ground. Here are some examples:

'As Henry VIII said to each of his wives in turn, "I shall not keep you long".'

'Your chairman just asked me, "Would you like to speak now, or should we let the guests enjoy themselves a little longer?"'

'The last time I made a speech, someone at the rear shouted, "I can't hear you!" – and a man sitting next to me yelled back, "I'll change places with you!"'

'Ladies and gentlemen, and any lawyers (or whatever) in the audience. . .'

'I feel like the young Arab Sheik who inherited his father's harem. I know exactly what to do, but where on earth do I start?'

'What can I say about James that hasn't been said in open court?'

'I'm only going to speak for a few moments because of my throat – if I go on too long, your president has threatened to cut it.'

'For the benefit of our honoured guests, let me introduce myself. My name is John Bowden. I'm here to help you through your after-dinner nap.'

'This is the first time I have spoken at such a convention, except during other people's speeches.'

'I'd like to thank you all for coming... especially those of you who knew I was going to say a few words but turned up anyway.'

'Ladies and gentlemen, last year when I was awarded the George Cross, the MBE and the Oscar for Best Actor... is an excellent way for a civil engineer to open a speech. It's a pack of lies of course, but it's an excellent way to open a speech.'

'In the interests of political correctness, this speech will contain nothing controversial or embarrassing about Peter, but instead will refer only to the nice, pleasant side of his character... Thank you and good afternoon.' *(Make as if to sit down.)*

'Thank you, Mary, for that introduction. If I'd known I was going to be that good, I'd have got here earlier to get a better seat.' *(After a glowing introduction.)*

Topical reference

A speaker who opens with a reference to a current event, news item or some other piece of interesting, topical information will be perceived as flexible and unconventional. At the same time, the audience will believe this speech was written specifically for them, because an identical one could not possibly have been delivered before.

'CNN has just broken the news that...'

'In the *Guardian* today it is reported that...'

'Within the last hour the Prime Minister has announced that...'

However, your reference need not be to national or international news. People are interested in events which impact directly upon them:

> 'Ladies and gentlemen, we have hit the target. I heard just as we came into the meeting. . .'

If you intend to make a topical opening, do not rely on fortune supplying you with just the right headline on the lunchtime news, or your chairman feeding you with a titbit of information as you stand up to speak. You would be wise to have a well-rehearsed back-up handy, should you need it. For example, you could devise a reserve topical opening based on the composition of the audience:

> 'More than 1,000 years of waste management experience is sitting in this hall. Each of you, 100 in all, has an average of ten years' experience. If you add mine, that makes 1,030.'

Silence

Opening in silence? This may sound a contradiction in terms. Yet it was a technique used effectively in a British Telecom advertisement to highlight the frustration of a person awaiting a phone call from a relative. A business speaker could use the same powerful device. Pause for five seconds before speaking:

> 'That was how long it seems to customers waiting for Technical Support to answer the telephone – and it's too long.'

A variation would be to do something unexpected, in silence. For example, you could walk to the front of the stage, take a five pound note from your pocket and slowly tear it in two:

> 'Some people in this company think money grows on trees. It doesn't seem to matter how much they waste so long as it doesn't belong to them.'

Displaying a visual aid in silence can focus an audience on a key aspect of your message. Use a bright, intriguing, simple caricature or illustration, preferably without supporting words. When you begin to speak, do not immediately refer to it. Allow explanation and spontaneous enlightenment to occur as the speech proceeds.

Consider other ideas too. There are so many new, exciting and unconventional openings. Look for a method that fits your personality. Test your opening. Have you used just the right words, in the right order, with the right timing? If you can leave it out altogether and it's not a loss, look for a better one. Then *memorise* and *practise* it. Rehearse, rehearse and rehearse. If your first sentence does not make an impact, you will lose your chance for immediate success. You only have one chance to make a good first impression.

PROVIDING A ROUTE MAP

Once you have hooked your audience with a self-interest, thought provoking, hard hitting or unusual opening – you should set the scene by clearly stating your **topic** and **theme**, and perhaps the reason for the speech. If necessary, define the limits within which you will work. Otherwise some people may be thinking about aspects of the subject which concern them, but do not necessarily concern you.

Use this second part of your opening to preview the speech. Lay out in summary form its structure. Provide a route map.

Opening with a hook

'The best way to predict the future is to create it. In today's competitive marketplace, it's not enough to build a better mousetrap; the world won't beat a path to your door. You must build them a motorway. The need for an overall marketing plan is acute. . .'

Following-up with a route map

'And that plan has to have three parts: Research your market. . . Position yourself against your competitors. . . Then develop a promotional plan to highlight your uniqueness. During the next 30 minutes you will learn how to create your future. . .'

Using a visual aid

Many speakers use a visual aid to show the structure of their speech in the form of sub-messages. If you do so, read it aloud, put it to one side and continually refer to it throughout your speech.

ENDING ON THE RIGHT NOTE

The conclusion of a speech is as big an opportunity as the opening, probably bigger. People remember the longest the last thing they hear. A bad ending can ruin even the best speech; a good ending can salvage even a mediocre one. Yet the majority of speakers just fade away when they get to the end of their speeches.

> **Powerful speakers conserve a lot of energy and concern for the audience until the end and make the conclusion their dessert, something delicious with a memorable aftertaste.**

The paradox is that you need to look backwards while at the same time pushing your audience forward to some sort of action. You need to bring the speech to a climax. You need to *sound* as if you have finished. But at the same time you want your listener to say 'You're right! I *will* do something about it.' Advertisers refer to this as the **target response** – what they want people to think, believe, feel or do as the result of what they have seen and heard.

The ending, like the opening, is too important to be left to the mercy of chance or the whim of the moment. It does not have to be long and complicated – indeed, it should not be – but it does have to be worked out in advance and well rehearsed. Don't say anything new. Don't simply paraphrase – which is to tread water. Remember your intended outcome. The conclusion must move your listener forward towards that outcome.

Creating a good close

A good close should fulfil three purposes. It should:

- Pull people together: producing the feeling that a common experience has been shared.

- Reinforce your central message: creating the image or thought you want to leave etched in your audience's mind.

- Be a call to action: motivating them to think or do something differently or better, as the desired outcome requires.

Here are two techniques to assist you achieve these objectives.

Making the sum more than the parts
Repeat the sub-messages, but give them an extra dimension, such as a mnemonic, slogan, rhyme or even a quotation bringing the individual parts together. Synergy can take the argument that one, essential step forward.

Changing your style
Even the most lucid presentation can benefit from a dramatic, passionate ending, providing, of course, the drama and passion are seen as relevant to the argument. But drama and passion are only partly in the performance. Eloquence demands the appropriate language, a sense of poetry. Suddenly the importance, relevance and significance to the listener of what he has already heard become more acute.

Ending with a flourish

There are many ways to conclude a speech. However, remember that every speech needs its *own* ending, tailored to its content, participants, atmosphere and to your desired outcome. The following list therefore is intended as no more than a broad spectrum of possibilities.

Challenging your audience
End on a positive, upbeat note. It's over to you.

> 'Now that I have shared my experiences with you, I ask every one of you to look deep inside your souls and ask yourself: Can we allow this situation to continue?'

Summarising the sub-messages
Have no more than three points. If you present more at the end of a speech, the summary will lose clarity and impact.

> 'Let me leave you with this thought: we face a three-way choice as we enter the new millennium, expand, export or expire.'

Suggesting agreement and recommending specific action
As would a lawyer before the jury retires.

> 'So those are the possibilities open to us. Only one of them carries any hope of real success. Can we agree that it is the duty of this board to protect and to advance the interests of all our shareholders by adopting it?'

Presenting a key statistic
People are generally turned off by too many facts and figures. However, one or two key statistics, held back until the end of a speech, can be highly effective, putting things into perspective.

> 'Let me close with some interesting figures. When Poland is admitted to the EU, the current market of ten million potential buyers of our products will grow to over 50 million. If we're serious about being a major player in that market, the time to aggressively expand our efforts is now.'

Telling them a story
Bob Monkhouse found the ideal ending to an after dinner speech

where the guest of honour was a millionaire well known for his left-wing politics and outspoken honesty about himself.

'Len uncorked a jeroboam of Don Perignon, and poured me a mugful. "Len," I said, "what is your political philosophy; what do you consider the purpose of government?" Unhesitatingly, and very earnestly, he replied, "The greatest good for the greatest number." "And what," I asked, "do you consider to be the greatest number?" And Len said, "Number one"... Ladies and gentlemen, the toast is.. Number One!'

As Mr Monkhouse points out, a very similar tale had been told about the scholar and philosopher David Hume 200 years earlier. Don't feel bound by factual accuracy. If you can find an apposite line by Dr Johnson, Voltaire or Genghis Khan, make a few minor adjustments here and there, and put it in the mouth of your managing director.

Going back to the future
This is a motivational close, generally expressing confidence that a job will be well done in the weeks and months that lie ahead.

'We are impressed with you... your hard work... your knowledge ... your skill... your drive. History tells us we have the competitive edge – a superior sales team that goes out every day to make it happen. That's history. And we have every confidence that it will be the future, thanks to each of you.'

Adapting good openings
In the first part of this chapter we discussed several approaches that also make good conclusions. However you end, remember that your last remarks will linger in the mind a little more than what went before.

Having the last word

Whenever possible, avoid ending a presentation with a questions and answers session. If you intend to take questions towards the end of the speech, you will need to prepare *two* closes: one to follow the body of your speech, and one as an encore after the Q&A session.

When you have tested your close (or two closes) and established that it really is the optimal one, *learn it by heart*. It is crucial to the effect of your entire speech and it must be perfect. This applies to the opening and closing of your speech, but *only* to them. Familiarise yourself with the rest of your speech, but do not even attempt to memorise it.

The conclusion, then, is the highlight of your speech, your final burst. Plan it well and practise it. The last sentence must come out perfectly. It is the last impression you leave with your audience.

BRACKETING A SPEECH

Bracketing is a device associated with *professional* speakers; it is rarely even attempted by *public* speakers. Bracketing provides the ultimate set of verbal bookends, because they match. The idea is to begin with an opening designed not only to grab an audience's attention at the *start* of a speech, but also – and at the same time – to set up a situation that can be exploited at the *end*. In this way you present your speech as a satisfying whole. The two brackets consist of a **set up** at the opening of the speech and a **pay off** at the end.

Many lyricists use this trick, establishing a phrase at the outset and repeating a variation of it to round off the last line. This is how Sammy Cahn achieved a nice little twist in the tail of *Call Me Irresponsible*:

> 'Call me irresponsible, call me unreliable, throw in undependable too.' *(Set up.)*

> 'Call me irresponsible, yes I'm unreliable, but it's undeniably true: I'm irresponsibly mad for you.' *(Pay off.)*

Brackets can serve you well in a speech. The words you will end with are planted clearly at the start, like this:

> 'Today, I confess that I've been daydreaming – both reminiscing about the past and predicting the future. We're celebrating a birthday, an anniversary. This company was founded exactly 30 years ago.' *(Set up.)*

> 'At the end of my reminiscing, I've come to these conclusions: We have done much for this company, and this company has done much for us. You have a right to be proud as managers. Let's congratulate ourselves and then move on to the next 30 years.' *(Pay off.)*

Notice how the repetition of the words *reminiscing, company* and *30 years* helps the open-and-closed nature of the brackets and provides a pleasing symmetry. Do not simply repeat your opening. This can easily happen if you follow the old 'tell them what you are going to tell them' approach. By all means use the same or similar material, but give it some memorable and appropriate twist. It is vital that the argument has developed. Merely putting the listener back to where he started will convey the impression that you have wasted his time.

QUESTIONS AND ANSWERS

Do I have to begin my speech with 'Ladies and Gentlemen', by saying 'Good morning', or by introducing myself?

No. That will waste those critical first moments of your speech. You can do this, if need be, in your second or third sentence.

Similarly, do I have to end with a 'Thank you'?

No. Your last words are critical. Do not waste them on pleasantries. It is never necessary to thank them for listening. However, sometimes it can be useful to thank them for their achievements. Under the right circumstances, this can make a very effective close: 'Thank you for your remarkable commitment, your exceptional performance and magnificent results. Keep it up.'

Can I reveal my conclusion at the beginning of a speech?

Yes. Think about the films and books that start at the end. Orson Welles' famous 'Rosebud' deathbed scene at the start of *Citizen Kane* is a classic example. Such an opening builds suspense as readers and viewers wonder how this ending came about. You can use this same technique to create anticipation in your audience: 'Yes, we should open our store for 24 hours a day'. Then discuss the pros and cons of the case before explaining precisely why you came to this conclusion.

CASE STUDIES

Timothy makes the board bored

Timothy, a head of department, presents a six-monthly report to the board meeting. He opens with what he considers to be a no-nonsense factual, logical account of recent developments and current trends. It sounds as if he is reading from the appendices of a detailed report. He has forgotten, or perhaps has never appreciated, that members of the board are only human, and want to be entertained and have a laugh every now and then. Yet neither his opening, nor anything that follows, raise even the suggestion of a smile.

Peter tells them that the end is nigh

Peter is the chief executive of a local district council. Towards the end of a rather dry presentation on central government funding, he senses that interest is waning. He wins the audience back by subtly telling them that he has almost finished his remarks: 'I have just two more points to make, perhaps I may then take a couple of minutes to summarise.' Interest is immediately restored. He then reinforces his central message before coming to his prepared close.

Lennox achieves a verbal KO

Lennox is a sales director who wants to convey the message that 'sales success means knowing your customer'. He concludes his speech to company reps with these words: 'I want to leave you with one last comment from an acquaintance of mine. He said, "A sales job is easy. I just keep reminding myself that these are not real people – they're only customers." That observation comes from supersalesman, P.L. Mason.' Lennox walks away from the podium, then turns and adds a final word, '... unemployed.' This unusual and thought provoking close has real impact.

SUMMARY

- It is essential to find a compelling opening and a compelling close (two closes, if you intend to take questions towards the end of the speech).

- The opening and close(s) should be appropriate given the content and tone of the body of the speech.

- An opening should grab an audience's attention and motivate them to listen.

- An opening should include a route map of the speech content.

- A close should reinforce your central message.

- A close should highlight what you want the participants to think or do differently or better as a result of the speech.

- Memorise your opening and close.

- Strive to have the last word.

5
Adding Flair to Your Words

There is no specific and correct way to express thoughts. You have a choice of words, many with subtle variations of meaning and tone. You have a choice of word patterns that can create vivid pictures, touch the emotions and stay in people's minds. The language you use to convey content in a business speech is critical. If the language isn't right, the thought conveyed isn't right. If the thought conveyed isn't right, the message isn't right. If the message isn't right, the desired outcome cannot be achieved and the speech will have failed. Think of choosing *effective* rather than *correct* language.

This chapter will explain how you can get your message across effectively by means of the following techniques.

* demystifying the professions
* using imagery
* remembering rhythm
* keeping it flowing
* forcing yourself to edit.

Use language well and people will perceive you to be as powerful as the message you convey.

DEMYSTIFYING THE PROFESSIONS

You are a businessperson who is used to corporate terms. You employ financial, industrial and commercial idioms, and that is the language you are comfortable with. Fine, but the very moment you rise to talk to an audience, you also step onto a stage. When you open your mouth to speak, you enter a world where corporate terms take a back seat; where financial, industrial and commercial idioms become subservient to colourful, powerful, memorable English. The more you can accept this, the more successful you will be.

Everywhere, the higher you climb up in the hierarchy, the more time you spend speaking. Yet the more we speak, the less there is within our little ponds that we can speak about with confidence. Most of us have become experts, specialised in one activity. A professor in inorganic chemistry often cannot understand what a professor of organic chemistry is saying. Learning to become an economist today is like learning a foreign language in which you talk about a rational world which exists only in theory.

Breaking down the barriers

The idea that we have reached the end of history once each of us has a profession and is master of its jargon is absurd. Humans are no longer what they were when they invented the idea of a profession as a sort of secret society with a monopoly of knowledge. The language of your speech should *not* be dictated by scientific, technical, industrial, statistical or other professional jargon. Simplify and personalise such material, even when addressing an audience of experts familiar with the specialist terms. Break down the barriers which prevent you from sharing the thoughts, language and style of other professions. The term 'social exclusion' applies not only to the poor but also to all those whose mind-set is confined to a single profession.

USING IMAGERY

Imagery is the implanting of word pictures in listeners' minds to illustrate, illuminate and embellish a speaker's thoughts. Which of the two following rhetorical questions has the greater impact on you?

'Can we continue to allow so many hundreds of pedestrians to be killed on our roads every year?'

'How would you feel if the doorbell rang, you opened the door and there, at your feet, lay the dead body of your child?'

No contest. The first question may make you *think*. The second will make you *feel*. If you *tell* them they may *listen*; if you *show* them they will *pay attention*; if you *involve* them they will *react*. The purpose of imagery is not to decorate, but to assist the purpose of the speaker.

An image may move the argument forward more cogently than pure reason. Simile or metaphor may more clearly express your thought than bald prose. The reaction you seek is both surprise and familiarity. A paradox? Yes. It is not the shocking surprise that makes you scream 'Eureka!' in your bath. It is the satisfying surprise you feel at the denouement of an Agatha Christie play – a surprise that makes you smile and gently nod your head in acknowledgement of a job well done. It is the shock of recognition when two familiar, yet apparently unrelated, elements fit into place:

'Her eyes were like flaming chip pans.'

Painting word pictures

Give your speech a graphic quality, not by telling a story but by painting word pictures that allow an audience's own imagination to take over. Specific detail allows an audience to see the scenes you are describing. This means avoiding vague reference to 'food' and replacing them with 'pizzas' and 'kebabs'. Use adjectives that conjure up specific images and trigger the senses: a *spicy* curry, a *fruity* jelly, a *savoury* pudding.

Using warm words

Words are powerful. They conjure images, evoke emotions and trigger responses deep within us so we react, often without knowing why. So-called *warm* words make us feel secure and comfortable, while *cold* words leave us uneasy and unsure. Writer Henry James said the two most beautiful words in the English language are summer afternoon, because they evoke just the right emotions.

In the early days of instant coffee, advertisers got off to a bad start by stressing words like 'quick', 'time-saving' and 'efficient'. These are all words without warmth and feeling. Makers of fresh coffee fought back with warm, happy, appetising words like 'aroma', 'fresh' and 'tasty'. Makers of instant coffee soon learned the lesson and their product became 'delicious', 'rich' and 'satisfying'. Sales 'blossomed'. The rest, as they say, is history.

Once you get into the habit of looking at the emotional colouring of words, as well as their meanings, you will find yourself using the kind of language that puts listeners at ease and encourages them to react more favourably to your speeches and to you.

Selecting similes

A **simile** is like a love song. It proves nothing yet describes so much. It makes abstract ideas imaginable. Reach for vivid comparisons. Help your listeners understand and remember. Invent tomorrow's clichés.

- as delicate as a whisper
- as inflexible as an epitaph
- as cold as outer space.

Making use of metaphors

A **metaphor** is a pair of spectacles we wear in order to think more clearly. It extends our language as we transfer our thought processes from one set of words to another. Unlike a simile, it provides a *single* image, which must be viewed through bifocals:

- The sullen sky leaned against the rooftops.
- Trees marinated the morning mist.
- Thoughts wriggled in my head.

Engaging all the senses

Sensory details bring breadth and depth to your descriptions. Why? Because you want your audience to believe in your anecdotes, to feel they have left their seats for a few moments and are 'living' within the story. This can happen only if the world you describe has all the trappings of the real world. And the real world is a sensory experience.

Take the sense of smell. How could you use it to help describe a dislikeable character? Give him breath that smells of drains. A pleasant girl? Try lemon-scented hair. An elderly, well-to-do bridge-playing couple? The odours of cigars, mothballs and Earl Grey tea. Pepper your descriptions with sensory detail. It will bring your anecdotes to life like a shot of whisky in a cup of coffee.

REMEMBERING RHYTHM

A good speech, like a good song, needs a regular beat. It should have a rhythm of its own; peaks, troughs, crescendos and a climax. It should have a lyrical quality that is music to an audience's ears. Here are a few simple techniques that will add an almost magical, melodic quality to your speeches:

- the rule of three
- parallel sentences
- alliteration
- repetition
- impact words.

Let's take each in turn.

The rule of three

Lyricists know they must always include a simple yet memorable 'hook' in their songs (the part you can't stop humming). One of the most effective is a three-word, three-phase, or three-sentence hook: 'She loves you, yeah, yeah, yeah'. The best speechwriters use the same technique. People like to hear speakers talk to the beat of three:

> 'Things have changed a lot over the last fifty years: from the Home Guard to home computers, from Vera Lynn to Vera Duckworth, from ration cards to scratchcards.'

Three is a magic number for speech-makers. It doesn't sound quite so effective in twos and fours, but fives and sevens work almost as well.

Parallel sentences
Sentences that are parallel add a rhythmic beauty that helps an audience anticipate and follow equal ideas:

> 'To change is normal. Nothing is constant except change. Our interest rates change... Our clothes change... Our cars change... The face of our workforce changes... Our politics change... Our philosophies change... Even our cultures change. Change has become the status quo. Change is the only thing that's the same. That's normal.'

Alliteration

> 'Looking and loving our behaviours pass
> The stones, the steels and the polished glass.'

The repetition of sounds and syllables, usually at the beginning of words, can help create a mood or unite a section of script. Alliteration can make your speeches special and spellbinding:

> 'A generation ago we feared typhoid more than terrorists... cholera more than crack... and rickets more than redundancy.'

Repetition
If there is anything that is almost guaranteed to make an audience break out into spontaneous applause it is a repetition of strong, emotive words:

> 'We will fight, and fight, and fight again to save the party we love.'

However, use the wrong words and it will fall flat. How does this sound?

'We will tussle, and tussle, and tussle again to protect the party we are fond of.'

'She likes you, yes, yes, yes.'

It doesn't work, does it?

Impact words
Use any of these words and I guarantee you will discover how easy it is to get the results you want:

- discovery
- guarantee
- love
- proven
- safety
- we

- easy
- health
- money
- results
- save
- you.

'We' and 'you' are the most important words of all. When you talk to an internal audience, identify yourself with them: *we* must understand; *our* session; *we* know; *our* interest. When you address an external audience, make it abundantly clear that you are no more than a catalyst: they are the ones who must make the required changes in attitude, feelings or knowledge: *you* must understand; *your* session; *you* know; *your* interest. You cannot stir your audience up if you do not address it directly. Remember the five-to-one rule: Every time you hear yourself saying 'I', try to follow it with five 'wes' or with five 'yous'.

The seven Cs of speechmaking
Be:

- Clear: use straightforward, everyday language.

- Colourful: use words that create an impression or enhance meaning.

- Creative: play around with words and word order.

- Concrete: use specific, unambiguous examples and language.

- Correct: both factually and politically.

- Concise: stand up to be seen; speak up to be heard; sit down to be appreciated.

- Conversational: speak in your natural, innate style.

KEEPING IT FLOWING

Have you noticed how entertainers, politicians and TV presenters move easily and unobtrusively from one topic to another? Like them, you can make your speech flow smoothly and gracefully from beginning to end.

Making transitions
Make use of a few of these simple devises of transition:

* bridges
* triggers
* rhetorical questions
* flashbacks
* lists
* pauses
* physical movement
* quotations, anecdotes and jokes.

Let us briefly consider each in turn.

A bridge
This is a word that alerts an audience that you are changing direction or moving to a new thought:

> 'We completed the project in July. *Meanwhile* other developments were taking place. . .'

> 'That was bad enough. *However*, there was even worse to come. . .'

> 'The results were significant. *But* the board was not convinced. . .'

A trigger
This is a repetition of the same word or phrase to link one topic with another:

> 'That was what the debtor situation was *like* in December. Now I'll tell you what it is *like* today. . .'

A rhetorical question
Asking a *rhetorical question* is another way of subtly changing direction:

> 'That's what a change of image can do for a company. So how can we improve our image?'

A flashback
A sudden shift to the past breaks what seems to be a predictable narrative:

> 'Today we are the market leader. *But three years ago* it wasn't like that. . .'

A list
A very simple way of combining apparently unrelated elements:

> 'We had four attempts to solve the problem. . .'

But don't overuse lists because a catalogue of events soon becomes extremely tedious to listen to.

A pause
This is a non-verbal method of showing your audience that you have finished a section of your speech and are about to move on to another.

Physical movement
Like a pause, movement, perhaps towards a flip chart, suggests you are moving on to something new.

A quotation, anecdote or joke
These can serve as excellent links. This example uses a joke from Bob Monkhouse:

> 'A strong employer deserves a strong union, and vice versa. If one of them is weak, both can suffer. Your chairman told me the story of one job applicant who said, "I like the job, sounds fine, but the last place I worked paid more, gave more overtime, more bonuses, subsidies, travel allowances, holidays with pay and generous pension schemes." Sir David said, "Why did you leave?" He said, "The firm went broke." That's the trouble with hard bargains – they can turn out to be hard on everyone. . .'

Influential phrases

Uncertain phrase	*Influential phrase*
• I think we should	• You should
• What I would like to propose	• I propose
• I will try to answer that	• Here's the answer
• I would like to summarise now	• In summary
• We may wish to consider	• You should consider

• I'll try to explain how	• Here's how
• We might be able to	• You can
• Can we talk about.	• Let's discuss.

FORCING YOURSELF TO EDIT

A speech is like a pair of shoes. It will always benefit from a little more polishing. Editing paves the way towards perfection. **Hold it two weeks** is a classic rule in advertising. For the speechwriter this may not be practicable. However, once you have completed your first draft, try to forget about it for a few days, if time permits, and then re-read it *out loud*. As you do so, ask yourself:

• Is it conversational?
• Is it concise?
• Does it have emotional appeal?

Is it conversational?
Do not fall into the trap of treating your draft as a literary exercise. Casual conversation is not constructed in a literary way. Choose your words carefully but communicate them in your natural, innate style. The quiet magnetic attraction of an assertive personality, of latent power, of sheer presence, is irresistible to any audience.

Is it concise?
Don't suffer from the illusion that you can make your speech immortal by making it everlasting. In the Bible, the Ten Commandments consist of 300 words (that's about two minutes speaking time), the story of the Creation is covered in 400 and the Lord's Prayer in 60. Yet the European Union Regulation on the import of caramel products has no less than 27,000 words (that would take you about three hours to chew over). Really important messages *can* be expressed in a few words – if you get to the point quickly.

As you edit, cut out the fat. There is one caveat: Do not cut helpful redundancy. If the repetition helps the listener to keep on track, think twice – and then a third time – before removing it. Cut in the same way as you think. And think as a listener.

Does it have emotional appeal?
Your speech should be an appeal to all the senses. It should *involve* your audience. It should allow them to do far more than just listen to you. It should allow them to *hear*, to *see*, to *smell*, to *touch*, to *taste*.

It should allow them to *experience* your words. When Isaac Newton was asked how he saw things so clearly, he said: 'I stand on the shoulders of men like Galileo.' Good speakers stand on the shoulders of Shakespeare, Churchill, Nelson Mandella, Mahatma Ghandi, JFK and Martin Luther King.

Applying the blue pencil
Judge for yourself what editing does for this speech excerpt:

Before editing

> 'Most successful sales representatives today appreciate that progress comes from having a detailed plan. They do not look to others for their leads. They do not blame support staff for lack of service or complain about inadequate sales literature. They are the accountable ones. They are responsible for the plan and they must achieve the results. Because of this, they are the ones who deserve the credit.'

After editing

> 'Successful sales reps like you know progress comes from having a detailed plan. You don't look to others for leads. You don't blame support people for lack of service. You don't complain about poor sales literature. You are accountable. You feel responsible for your plan. You must achieve the results. You deserve the credit.'

A great improvement, I'm sure you will agree.

QUESTIONS AND ANSWERS

How can I learn to create powerful and effective metaphors?

Try experimenting with nouns and verbs. Get a sheet of paper. Write a list of nouns down the left side and a list of verbs down the right. Anything will do: Tables, computers, storms, soap, saxophones; falling, boiling, dressing, dancing, drinking. Now mix and match the verbs with the nouns, looking for combinations that strike you as piquant, and put them into sentences.

The trick is to focus on secondary characteristics. When we think of 'boiling', for example, the first thing that comes to mind is 'heat' and 'steam'. What else does boiling do? It 'melts' things, turning them into liquid. So if we combine 'boil' with 'storm', for example, we might come up with: 'The storm boiled the ground into instant mud pudding.' Result: An instant and powerful image of a quagmire. With a little practice, you will find a new world of linguistic possibilities opening up for you.

What is the best way to build up a personal thesaurus of original similes?

Make a list of common descriptive similes and then rewrite each with one or two alternative comparisons. For example, 'quiet as a lamb' could become 'quiet as a locked door' or 'quiet as a Celtic supporter at the Rangers' end.' Start with these: Slow as a tortoise; clean as a whistle; sick as a parrot. Once you get used to rewriting similes, start creating your own, from scratch: Icebergs as tall as cathedrals; suave as a row of head waiters; inconspicuous as the Invisible Man. Now, over to you: Music. . .; profitable. . . ; dynamic. . . .

Are there any other special linguistic devises I can use to add a sparkle to my speeches?

Here are some more figures of speech. They are really for speakers who have reached the supreme champion stage:

- Hyperbole. Exaggeration for effect: 'I've told you millions of times not to exaggerate.'

- Irony. The meaning is conveyed by words whose literal meaning is the opposite: 'Don't worry. It doesn't matter if we lose the order and our jobs.'

- Antithesis. Contrasting thoughts are placed side by side for emphasis: 'Some rise by sin and some fall by virtue.'

- Paradox. A statement which on first hearing seems absurd or contradictory, but isn't: 'I'm sorry this speech is so long; I didn't have enough time to make it shorter.'

- Oxymoron. Two contradictory terms are combined to form a phrase: 'It was a bitter-sweet experience.'

- Zeugma. A verb is applied to two nouns, though strictly appropriate to only one of them: 'We sang their songs and their praise.'

- Personification. Inanimate or abstract objects are treated as though they were human: 'The factory breathes new life.'

Don't overdose. Technique must not get in the way of the message. It must assist and, if possible, enhance it.

CASE STUDIES

Patrick simply doesn't simplify

Patrick is a senior management accountant who has been asked to give a presentation on cost structures to an audience of mixed knowledge and experience. He begins his speech as follows:

> 'Cost structures are affected by a wide variety of factors. Demand profiles and cost structures, for example, are directly correlated by an R-squared of 0.85. The normal histogram necessitates split shifts and spreadover payments in addition to USH payments with load factors, particularly at the shoulders. Then you've got the problem of dead mileage and excessive layover which is fine for TPOs on DMUs but poor for allocations and TMs.'

Patrick makes just about every mistake possible regarding his choice of words.

- He has an abstract beginning. Very few people can think in formal or abstract terms outside their own field of expert knowledge. It is better to open with a concrete example.

- He uses unexplained technical language. 'Correlated' may be understood, but how many people will be familiar with 'R-squared'?

- He uses undefined jargon: 'split shifts', 'spreadovers', 'dead mileage', 'layover'.

- He uses technical terms that have different meanings in everyday life: 'shoulders', and even 'histograms'.

- He uses undefined acronyms: 'USH', 'TPOs', 'DMUs', 'TMs'.

Majid avoids the abstract

Majid is asked to address a European financial services industry technology conference. His topic is customer databases. Majid appreciates that his listeners are not experts and could find the subject complex and dull. The benefits could easily be too abstract for many of them to grasp easily. The subject needs to be made human. He begins his speech in this manner:

> 'What's a database? Well here's mine (*he holds up his pocket diary*). No, it's not a filofax. . . it's my diary. It's easy to access, concise, well laid out, and that simple diary tells me what I need to know. That's what my database does. It's a store of information.

My personal database is on paper but it could just as well be on disk, or anything else.'

He carries on in this vein. He makes the abstract tangible, and it works.

Mary gets on her bikes

Mary is a senior research chemist working for a multinational pharmaceutical company. She is asked to talk to the main board about a new drug and its market competitors. Mary's dilemma is that some of the board members are highly qualified and experienced scientists, while others have very little knowledge of chemistry. She comes up with the idea of opening with a visual aid. In silence she turns on the overhead projector to reveal a slide showing three bicycles: a penny farthing, a mountain bike and the machine Chris Boardman pedalled to gold at the Olympic Games. Immediately the audience sit up. What has this to do with chemistry?

After a few seconds, Mary points out that these bikes have a lot in common: two wheels, pedals, a saddle. But look how different they are too: size, gears, aerodynamics. She goes on to develop this analogy of similarities and differences by superimposing the molecular structure of the new drug alongside the Boardman bike and those of its competitors alongside the older bikes. Once again, she first discusses similarities before turning to the fundamental and important differences between the molecular structures. The experts in the room are in no way patronised by this thoughtful and unusual approach – and it makes all the difference to those present who are not trained scientists. After the presentation, the financial director is heard to reflect: 'Why wasn't chemistry taught like that in school?'.

SUMMARY

- Demystify the professions.
- Use vivid imagery.
- Remember rhythm.
- Keep it flowing.
- Edit.

6
Delivering a Speech

Most of the traditional advice on how to speak and present in public is out of date and, in many respects, it is wrong. True, a little judicious advice can smooth the edges without stifling individuality. Yet a great deal of so-called expert advice will remove the wonderfully imperfect distinctions about us and create unremarkable clones. The world has moved on. Attitudes have changed; people have changed. The days of the obligatory Oxbridge news presenter are gone forever.

This chapter will *not* put you in a straitjacket of artificial presentation techniques. You will not be told how to stand, how to gesticulate, how to look at people, how to talk. In everyday life you have no trouble with any of these skills, and the combinations in which you use them make up your personality. If you abandon everything that is natural to you and substitute 'acquired' mannerisms, is it really surprising that you will come over as unnatural, awkward and insincere?

When you stand up to speak, you need to do three things:

- be conversational
- project your personality
- be heard.

These goals may sound glaringly obvious, yet few speakers even consider them.

BEING CONVERSATIONAL

When you are sitting leisurely, with family, friends or colleagues, your conversation will be naturally relaxed and chatty, because that is the language of easy communication. When you make a business speech, the words and phrases you use should be more considered, imaginative, creative and rhythmical than your everyday language. Yet the way you say them, the way you deliver your speech, should remain unaffectedly relaxed and chatty.

Being yourself

If you are different from your usual self you may be perceived as phoney, boring, or lacking in personality. As a result, people will not take to you and they certainly will not be convinced by, or remember, much of what you have to say. Certainly you may need to speak a little louder or make other concessions to accommodate the needs of your audience, but in essence nothing in your delivery style should change. You should be yourself made large.

> **The key is to recognise what you are doing when you get it right and achieve *any* successful communication, be it formal or informal, business or social, and then stay with it.**

You need to recognise, and then capture, this normal style of communication and make it work for you, naturally, and in any given situation, regardless of the stress level. When you walk into your office, a restaurant or a greengrocer's shop, you don't hover outside anxiously rehearsing how you will deliver your lines. We all communicate each day without fear of failure. If you can understand how normal, relaxed, informal spoken communication works, you will be able to understand what you must do, and keep on doing, during formal spoken communication.

So what are the critical elements of normal conversational communication which allow people to transmit and receive information effortlessly when they are relaxed and operating in a low stress environment? Analyse the differences between your casual conversation and your current presentation style.

The way you sound

Most of us are astonished the first time we hear our own voice. The resonant sounds we've heard in our heads seem thin and alien issuing from an audio or video player. It doesn't matter. Think about some of our top personalities and most effective communicators: Melvyn Bragg, Joan Bakewell, Peter Snow, Kate Adie, Jonathan Dimbleby, Jeremy Paxman. None of these gifted talkers would win prizes at RADA. There is nothing of the mighty orator about any of them. All these famous and successful individuals stopped worrying about their voices long ago, if they ever did. They are each concerned with putting across their ideas. They speak to us with conviction, sincerity, urgency – and sometimes fun.

It doesn't matter whether speakers have unusual accents or even speech impediments, as long as people can *understand* them. Paradoxically, an unusual accent or speech problem can often help to reinforce a message by making it seem real and natural. From the moment you utter your famous first words you are testing different ways of catching people's attention and achieving what you want. All through your life you continue to build on those skills. Your conversational abilities are far more practised than your literary abilities. Casual conversation is not constructed in a literary way. You do not always finish your sentences. You repeat yourself. You use ungrammatical constructions – but you are obeying a different set of rules. You are obeying the rules of effective spoken communication which have been learnt, instinctively, down the ages. Don't abandon these rules when you speak in public.

Getting adequate feedback

Do not engage in a monologue. Adopting a conversational approach is not just about conveying information, or sharing emotions, or a way of putting ideas into people's heads. A conversational approach should encourage a genuine meeting of minds, each with different memories and habits. When minds meet, they do not simply exchange facts, they transform them, re-shape them, draw different implications from them. A conversational approach to speechmaking should not just re-shuffle the cards, it should create new cards.

PROJECTING YOUR PERSONALITY

Your personality is your greatest asset. It is personal chemistry that makes people want to do business with other people. Very few of us, given the choice, will choose to work with someone we don't like or trust. If you are already successful to any degree the chances are that you have a 'winning personality'. The challenge is to project it, not suppress it. If you succeed, you will feel comfortable and at ease. If you feel comfortable, your audience will feel comfortable and become receptive, open and focused. Mutual comfort is the key to assimilation and acceptance.

Each speaker is unique; each speaker has a unique style. What might be most effective for one person would be a disaster for another. Think carefully about what *you* are doing when you communicate effortlessly under everyday circumstances. Probably you will not have considered this before. It is an extremely useful exercise because it makes you appreciate what you must also do during your speeches. In particular think about:

- the way you act
- the way you look.

The way you act

When a person talks informally, he probably sits or stands in a relaxed manner, breathing naturally, maintaining an appropriate level of eye contact, gesturing every now and then to reinforce his words, and smiling at intervals to establish and maintain rapport. Yet the moment this same person stands up to address an audience, he becomes nervous, distrusts his innate powers of communication and relies on a range of artificial presentation techniques.

We all want certainties to cling to when we are entering uncharted waters, which is why people visit astrologers – and speech trainers. I'll leave you to decide about astrologers, but much advice proffered by speech trainers is patently ludicrous: pushing your shoulders back throughout the speech; counting to six as you breathe in through the nose and to four as you push air out from the diaphragm; maintaining eye contact for at least eighty-four – yes eighty-four per cent of the presentation; exaggerating every gesture by one quarter; and smiling throughout. These are all genuine pieces of advice given by eminent trainers, and they are all very silly.

The moment you are told to do something in a certain way you become conscious of what you should be doing naturally. You have given yourself one more thing to think about, when all you should be thinking about is:

- conveying the right message
- and achieving the desired outcome.

The way you look

The objective of this book is to help speakers achieve or exceed their objectives. You must be outcome-centred in your results focus, but audience-centred in your delivery. Personal appearance has a major impact on how you are perceived by that audience. I would not presume to say any more about the way you dress or groom yourself, but would suggest you consider objectively what a powerful part of your assessment of others this is, and act appropriately.

Getting back to basics

Once you accept that you can approach even the most daunting speech in exactly the same way as you approach informal communication, your apprehension will dwindle and your confidence will soar. Knowing that you not only *can*, but also *should* 'be yourself' will stop you worrying about your performance, and allow you to concentrate on what really matters: message and outcome.

BEING HEARD

You must be *audible*. If you are not, all else is lost. If there is public address equipment available, find out how it works, get plenty of practice and then use it. Don't trust in luck and don't believe people who tell you to leave it all to them. Accept personal responsibility. You are the one who will look awkward if things go wrong.

If there is no sound-enhancing equipment, speak as clearly and as loudly as is necessary to be heard. If the only other person in the room was at the back, you would talk to him naturally, at the right level, without shouting or strain, by:

- keeping your head up
- opening your mouth wider than during normal speech
- using clearer consonants
- slowing down.

If you remember that you must be heard by that same man, at the back, during your speech, however many other people may be in the room, you will make those same four *natural* adjustments to your delivery. However, and contrary to conventional wisdom, if you make a conscious effort to talk more slowly simply because you are in front of an audience, regardless of whether the farthest listener is 3 or 30 metres away, your delivery will sound unnatural and artificial. It doesn't matter whether you talk quickly or slowly, as long as you are speaking at the same rate as you would do if talking only to that man at the back.

QUESTIONS AND ANSWERS

How well should I rehearse my delivery?

Rehearse your opening and close until you have them spot on. Rehearse the body of your speech not to be *perfect*, but to be *comfortable*. Audiences don't care if you're perfect, but they will only be comfortable if you are. And if they are not comfortable, they will not be receptive to your message.

What should I do if I make a mistake?

Admit it and move on. Humour often helps. This is not a turning point in Western civilisation. The world will continue unimpeded tomorrow. If you're comfortable, use your mistake to point out that we live in an imperfect world and the point isn't to be flawless, but to be accountable. Tell the audience that it is always better to be able to correct an error than be unaware of it. Customers who complain should always receive a polite and careful hearing because, not only might they be correct, but also they are potential long-term customers.

Should I ask an audience to evaluate my platform skills?

A speech is a means to an end. It is not an end in itself. Dr Albert Bandura, one of the pre-eminent psychologists of our time, has shown that people with low self-perceptions of their knowledge and abilities put a premium on external performance standards to reassure themselves of their accomplishment. People with high self-perceptions of their knowledge and abilities place the emphasis on the *outcome* of their endeavours.

CASE STUDIES

Lee is not himself
Lee is an American investment banker based in London. He is called upon to give a talk on the bond market and syndication of debt issues. Although the content of his presentation is excellent, his presentation is ineffective because he puts on an act – an act influenced by his perception of how a smart, young Wall Street banker *should* talk. This is entirely foreign to his natural style and consequently he comes over as shallow and insincere.

Joseph tries too hard
Joseph, the chairman of a multinational textile manufacturing company, is interviewed on a major business television programme. He is overly cautious in the way he expresses himself, working too intently to give perfectly packaged, grammatical answers to every question. He comes across as patronising and diffident, and seems to be talking down to the interviewer and the viewers when in fact, under less stressful circumstances, he is one of the most personable, approachable and effective communicators imaginable.

Tony gets a pleasant surprise
Tony is a world-famous British chief executive who gives a very informative speech to fifty of his French colleagues. He has practised the contents, as well as the French intonation and expression very carefully. The reception he receives is extremely warm and friendly. When

he asks what has specifically impressed his audience, the answer comes as a surprise to him: his smile, charm, elegance and wit – not the sophisticated contents of the speech or his immaculate French accent and pronunciation. Win the heart and the head will follow.

SUMMARY

- Do not put on an act.
- Analyse the difference between your casual conversational style and your current presentation style.
- Be conversational.
- Project your personality, don't suppress it.
- Be yourself made large.
- Be heard.

7
Handling Questions

Questions. Some people love them. Some speakers hate them. Love them or hate them, you are probably going to get them. And as a speaker you need to know how to handle them. Questions should be taken as an opportunity to interact with your audience. They enable you to gauge whether they are following you, understanding your argument and agreeing with what you say. They provide valuable feedback.

Questions turn a monologue into a dialogue, a meeting of minds.

Is it always wise to invite questions during a presentation? If you suspect that some or any of the audience are out to damage you, it would be foolish to offer them the opportunity to do it publicly. It is perfectly reasonable to offer to answer questions individually and informally after the speech. Consider the purpose of the speech: if it is to entertain, welcome or say farewell, questions are superfluous to the occasion. The size of the audience is another factor to consider. The larger the audience the more inhibiting it is to potential questioners. There is a feeling of why me and not one of the 499 others? Also, they may remain silent if they believe their question is only relevant to ten per cent of the audience. With audiences in the hundreds questions are rarely a good idea.

Using questions positively

These are exceptions. Most business speeches elicit questions. They are an integral part of the entire presentation. Audiences expect them as a right. Organisers demand them. You should welcome them as a method to encourage interaction and to take the focus away from yourself for a brief moment. You can use questions to reinforce your central message and help you achieve your overall objective. Handled properly, question time can underline your authority. This chapter considers:

- timing question sessions
- preparing for question sessions
- conducting question sessions
- handling difficult questions
- dealing with difficult questioners.

TIMING QUESTION SESSIONS

An audience's attention fluctuates significantly throughout a speech, as illustrated by Figure 7 on page 52. The basic pattern is one of heightened attention at the beginning, followed by lower attention throughout the main content (unless you inject occasional points of particular interest), and culminating with a rise in both attention and retention at the end. What does this tell us about when to handle questions?

Broadly, the options are inviting questions:

- after the speech
- during the speech
- before the summary.

After the speech

This is the most common method employed by speakers. It is also the poorest. By turning the final part of your presentation over to your audience, you run the risk of having them leave the room remembering your difficulty in answering an embarrassing or tricky question. There's also the danger that someone will attempt to hijack the event by asking an irrelevant question or raising an issue which undermines your entire case. This format also denies feedback throughout the speech and may allow a serious mismatch to develop between the message you *think* you are getting across and the message the audience is *actually* receiving.

During the speech

This problem of feedback is resolved when questions are asked throughout the speech, as and when questioners feel the need to ask them. And as this format requires active participation by the audience, another benefit is the heightened level of audience interest and retention that will occur. But there are difficulties, too. If you are on a tight schedule, lengthy questions may prevent you completing your speech on time. Unless the questions are relevant to the entire audience, some listeners may feel their time is being wasted and may lose interest. A premature question may also upset the way you had planned to present your material. It takes a great deal of skill to handle questions effectively during a presentation, and still maintain control and continuity.

After sections
The dilemma of feedback versus continual interruption can be overcome by inviting questions after each section of your talk. This method is particularly useful for a lengthy or complex presentation or lecture. It allows uninterrupted discussions, yet enables both speaker and audience to check that they are still in touch while there is still opportunity to put things right.

Differentiating between reasons for questions
One simple, effective way of allowing questions when they are most meaningful to the audience, while still keeping the speech on track, is to differentiate between *clarification* and *additional information*. This approach assures the audience that you will cover all their questions before the event is over, and also gives you the option of answering each question when posed or putting it on hold, as you see fit. Before you get into the main body of your speech, you could say, 'I will take questions which call for clarification at any time, but any questions which require additional information, or which relate to matters not directly covered in the speech will be dealt with towards the end.'

Before the summary
Notice the phrase 'towards the end.' There is an excellent compromise approach that you can use in cases where you have been told that the question period will come after rather than during the speech. Consider taking questions *after* the main part of your speech but *before* you present your summary and deliver your final round verbal KO. A simple statement like, 'I will be pleased to answer any questions you may have, but would like to hold the final two or three minutes for a summary', can give you all the control you need. You can use this time to recover from any possible irrelevant, embarrassing or critical questions, and to send the audience away with your ideas, not someone else's.

Setting the boundaries
Whenever you decide to accept questions, make this crystal clear immediately after your introductory remarks. Set the boundaries. 'I

will be pleased to answer questions for up to five minutes after each of the three sections of the presentation. I'm afraid we can't discuss X because of the pending litigation and we'll have to avoid the issues of Y and Z for security reasons.' Such comments at the outset set the stage for your control of what is to follow.

PREPARING FOR QUESTION SESSIONS

The ideal response to a question is to answer it well *and* relate it back to your main message *and* use it as a means of improving relations with your audience – all *apparently* spontaneously.

Anticipating questions

Try to anticipate likely questions. With a little thought, many questions can easily be predicted. Here are a few ways to jump-start your thought processes:

- consider generic questions
- review your audience analysis
- brainstorm
- plant and otherwise encourage questions.

Considering generic questions
There are certain generic questions that you should prepare a response for in almost every business setting.

- Benefit questions:
  - What will we gain by doing this?
  - What are the alternatives?
  - What is the risk if we don't do this?

- Action questions:
  - What steps should we take to implement your ideas?
  - Who will take responsibility for this project?
  - How long will it take?

- Cost questions:
  - How much will this cost?
  - How much do alternatives cost?

Reviewing your audience analysis
Because you have already analysed the audience in some detail, this part of question anticipation is easy. What would a typical person from this audience be likely to ask? By analysing the audience you

raise their natural biases in your mind and thus approach the topic
from their point of view. By doing so you will be more likely to
encourage the type of question you are prepared to answer.

Brainstorming
Having two or three other people with you in a room for 20 minutes
brainstorming questions will yield a far greater percentage of antici-
pated questions than you could ever generate by yourself. To conduct
such a session, let your colleagues know the speech topic and generally the nature of the audience. Give them an outline before the meeting and advise them what you hope to achieve. Tape record the
session. Review it directly after the meeting and draw up your list of
potential questions. If you leave it too long, you will lose momentum.

Planting and otherwise encouraging questions
It is a perfectly legitimate tactic to **plant** questions in the audience.
Prepare 'text-book' answers that reinforce your central message. Tell
your confederate to ask a question to start the ball rolling or to fill
in any embarrassing pregnant silence. If the question sessions comes
at the end of your slot, or just before a coffee break, set up a final
question which you can answer with great authority. Your audience's
attention will be at a natural peak, anticipating a change of stimulus,
and so you can lodge in their alert minds a strong and positive impression of your competence, and of your main message.

Alternatively, you could build a trailer into your speech: 'I don't
want to dwell on the issue of a possible European grant now. If any
of you has a special interest, we can find time at the discussion stage.'
If they bite, fine. If they don't you can give them the good news in
your summary.

Questioning yourself
Finally, why not in effect ask your own question? Many a seasoned
speaker does this and his audience hardly ever realises what's going
on:

> 'I heard some of you in the lobby discussing the reorganisation of
> accounts. It strikes me that this raises the issue of. . .'

> 'Your chairman picked me up at the railway station this morning
> so we could have a little time to discuss. . .'

> 'On reflection, perhaps I did not spell out the important implica-
> tions of the new Act. . .'

Reinforcing your message

Don't go as far as the politician who ignores the interviewer's questions and simply repeats and repeats his tub-thumping message. Answer each question on its merits, but phrase your response in terms of their relevance to your speech objectives. Try to hook your answer back to your message:

'Once again, I believe this emphasises our reliability.'

'And that's another example of us keeping to our word.'

'When we say a thing, we mean it.'

Ringing the changes

Arm yourself with another two or three memorable ways of expressing your central message. If you use the same turn of phrase over and over again, your credibility will suffer.

'Over the past five years we have lost:

– more customers than there were runners in the London Marathon;

– the equivalent of 13 customers for each person working here;

– enough customers to populate (a local village or suburb).'

Having enough spare ammunition

Always keep something in reserve for question time. This does not mean withholding a key element of your speech against the possibility of being asked an appropriate question. It does mean having spare examples, illustrations, statistics, anecdotes, slides, expert opinion which echo an argument or better still play to your main points:

'When British Gas tried this method they found that. . .'

'This is a graph showing. . .'

'Professor Higgins has concluded that. . .'

CONDUCTING QUESTION SESSIONS

How you conduct the question period can be one of the most significant factors in the success or failure of your speech. Accordingly, here are some key pointers to keep in mind.

Having a positive attitude

This is the most important single consideration. If you approach questions as if your audience were trying to put you on the spot or catch you out, you are bound to become defensive. If, on the other hand, you approach questions as if your audience were paying you a compliment by showing an interest in your topic, the difference in your relationship with your audience will be tremendous.

Functions of a question session

- It dramatically increases an audience's attention span and level of engagement.

- You can guage the feeling of the audience towards your speech.

- Points of detail can be clarified.

- Certain areas of presentation can be developed.

- It helps you build credibility and gain agreement on minor issues.

- It can be used to powerfully reinforce your message.

Treating questioners with respect

Always try to imply that a question is insightful and relevant, but avoid overusing stock phrases such as 'Good question' or 'I'm glad you asked that', as these may make you sound patronising. It often becomes necessary either to clarify exactly what information the questioner desires or to check your understanding of the question. A skilful speaker will do so without ever embarrassing the individual: 'Let me re-phrase that a little; you seem to be asking. . .'

Stages of a question session

- Change gear. Relax. Take a seat. Say, 'Now let's pause for a few moments while I get my breath back and you think about what questions you might want to ask.'

- Embrace the question. 'That's an interesting angle. Yes, we should explore that further.'

- Pay close attention, and signal courteous interest. Pause, and let them see you are thinking about the answer.

- If necessary, repeat the question to make sure you heard it correctly.

- If your answer has to be a long one, embrace the whole audience. Say, 'We can see, can't we, why Dr Black has asked that question?'

- Confirm that the questioner is satisfied with your response. 'Does that answer your question?'

Monitoring the audience's response

You can tell a great deal about what an audience is thinking by their reactions. Most people's response to your communication will be easy to read by watching their body language. They will nod their heads when they agree with you and frown, look away or shake their heads when they disagree. You need to watch your audience attentively, and try to understand what they are thinking. Do they agree or disagree? Are they interested or bored? If body language is negative, you still have a chance to have another go. Explain the point again, but this time make a particular effort to be clear and concise. Give an example or two, if it helps. If they continue to look uncertain, say: 'I see you remain unconvinced. Would someone be willing to voice the reasons for his doubts?'.

Concluding with a summary

Don't let your speech limp to a close after the last question. Retain control. Say, 'I have time for one or two more questions.' This allows you to end on a positive note. For example, if you are asked a weak or inappropriate question, or if you answer a good question poorly, you can simply take another. If, on the other hand, you do an exceptional job, you may want to look at your watch and say, 'I've taken enough of your time already. Perhaps I could now make a few final remarks before we close.' Conclude with your prepared closing remarks – that pithy quote or challenging question that will leave your audience charged up and ready to act.

HANDLING DIFFICULT QUESTIONS

There are certain questions that may be difficult to answer or may divert you from your message if they are not handled properly. Here are some that occur most frequently, together with some effective ways of handling them.

Typical problem questions

Problem
A question refers to a topic that you intend to cover later in your speech.

Solution
Provide a condensed answer, indicating that you will be providing more detail later. Don't worry about subsequently repeating a point, as this will reinforce your message. However, if possible use different words, expressions, anecdotes, examples and so on, in the abbreviated answer rather than in the main body of the speech:

> 'Thank you for raising that point. We are also most concerned about the environmental issues. We will not be building anything in that field. I'll be talking about this in detail after lunch. Perhaps you could ask your question again then if you feel any of your concerns have not been addressed.'

Problem
A question is diversionary and might lead to discussion away from your objectives.

Solution
Answer it briefly. Summarise where the discussion was prior to the question, in order to re-focus the audience on your message:

> 'Of course you are right; we must target the Scottish market. But, as I was explaining, there is little point in doing so until we improve the reliability of our after-sales service. . .'

Alternatively, take the blame yourself:

> 'Something I said must have led you off the subject; this is what we should be discussing. . .'

Problem
An apparently single question actually contains a series of possibly unrelated questions.

Solution
Do not attempt to answer the entire question with vague generalities. Ask the speaker to be more specific or to simply answer the part of the question that will best reinforce your message:

'Your point about employment training is particularly valid. Here's how we are going to handle that. . .'

Problem
The question is hypothetical:

'What would you do if. . .?'

Solution
Don't answer it. Say you would rather deal with factual questions:

'I would rather respond to factual situations about what is – than what could, might or should be.'

Problem
You are asked a question to which you do not know the answer.

Solution
Admit it and refer to someone who can answer or offer to find out the answer later and let them know. No one expects you to be omniscient. Bluffing is always a bad way out. Not only do you fail to satisfy the questioner, but you raise doubts with the audience about the truthfulness of your entire speech:

'Unfortunately I don't have a ready answer for that one. I'll talk to Roy who prepared the summary and get back to you this afternoon.'

Options for dealing with difficult questions

- Answer the question.
- Refuse to answer (explain why).
- Say you don't know, but will find out and let them know.
- Hold it for a moment until you have finished making a point.
- Defer answering until later in the presentation.
- Promise to deal with it privately after the speech.
- Refer it to an expert colleague.
- Throw it back to the person who asked it.
- Throw it to another member of the audience.
- Put it up for general discussion.

DEALING WITH DIFFICULT QUESTIONERS

Whenever you conduct a question session you run a risk. You may have some people in the audience with a personal agenda that may not contribute to your presentation objectives. You must develop skills for dealing with people who will attempt to use your question time for their own purposes. Here are some suggestions for dealing with the kinds of difficult questioner you are most likely to encounter.

The arguer
He insists on getting into a one-on-one debate on a particular topic.

Solution
He probably seeks recognition. Give it and then get on with your question period:

'You've raised some interesting points. I'd like to take time to explore them with you later.'

Don't get into an argument, you may win the battle but you will lose the war:

• He probably won't let go even when proved wrong.

• The rest of the audience will soon lose interest.

• If you make him look foolish, the rest of the audience may identify with him and resent you for it.

The devious and hostile
He is downright nasty and unpleasant.

Solution
It is possible to handle the situation without being aggressive or passive. Don't fight back. If you pick a fight with one audience member, you pick a fight with them all. Try to answer patiently – *once*:

'Perhaps there has been a misunderstanding. Let me try to clarify the situation...'

If the hostility continues, recognise it as such, and use the power of the group to your advantage, by saying:

'I don't think I'm able to satisfy you on that right now. Perhaps we can get together and talk it out later. Now rather than waste everybody's time, I'd like to take another question.'

The dominator
He lets you get the audience together and then tries to make his own speech to them.

Solution
Don't allow him to take over. Remember your objectives. Be polite but assertive:

'May we have your question please.'

The enemy
He doesn't like you and his questions reflect this.

Solution
Emphasise points of agreement and minimise differences. Or frankly ask that personalities be left out.

The heckler
He continually interrupts you – fortunately a rare occurrence during a business speech.

Solution
Make a witty reply, or give a serious answer, or carry on as if you hadn't heard him, or appeal for a fair hearing, or ask him to leave.

The inarticulate
He has the ideas, but cannot put them across.

Solution
Help him out by saying:

'Let me repeat that.' Then re-phrase his question.

The mistaken
He is clearly wrong, but just can't or won't see it.

Solution
Politely but firmly point out his error:

'That's one way of looking at it, but how can we reconcile that with (state the correct point)?'

Use the opportunity to explain your argument once again, from a slightly different angle.

The pig-headed
He absolutely refuses to accept points being discussed.

Solution
Tell him time is short, but that you would be glad to discuss it with him later.

The professional griper
He insists on making political points.

Solution
Politely point out that you cannot (or will not) change policy here; the objective is to operate as best we can under the present system.

The rambler
He talks about everything except the subject under discussion. If you allow him to drone on indefinitely you will lose valuable time as well as the interest of the rest of the audience.

Solution
Don't embarrass him. At a pause in his monologue, jump in and ask and answer the question for him:

'So you would like to know about the revised R&D programme. Let me tell you what we intend to do. . .'

The show off
His real motive is to show his colleagues how well informed he is. He seeks recognition. Nothing will make him happier than to have his expertise publicly commended. He is more interested in his question than in your answer.

Solution
Don't be afraid to tell him how clever he is. Prolonged discussion offers no benefits. The quicker you can get off the subject the better:

'You're right, of course. I was talking about the German sweet-meat market in general, not the German market for marshmallows, which obviously you know more about than I do.'

The status quoer
He is concerned that something you are proposing may mean a cut off in staff, budget, status, authority, patronage or perks:

'Does that mean there will be less overtime?'

Solution
With a difficult question of any kind, your first reaction should be to quell any emotional response you may find rising in your breast, and your second should be to explore the question and ask the questioner to elaborate and refine it. Don't get defensive. Put it in perspective. Describe some compensating benefit.

The tester
He intends to publicly probe your knowledge and experience:

'What was the bad debt provision last year?'

Solution
The golden rule is not to bluff or to try to excuse your ignorance. If you don't know, promise to find out for the questioner – and keep the promise.

Handling difficult questions

- Listen carefully right to the end.

- If necessary clarify, repeat or paraphrase.

- Decide why the question has been asked.

- Beware of assumptions.

- Separate the strands.

- Keep cool under fire.

- Never put down the questioner.

- Don't feel you must answer – there are always alternatives to a direct answer.

- Don't be abrupt.

- Don't go on for too long.
- Link your reply to your message.
- Make sure the questioner is satisfied with your reply.
- Thank the questioner, if only with a smile.

QUESTIONS AND ANSWERS

I've heard it said that it's a good idea to always pause for a moment before answering a question. Do you agree?

Yes. There are four good reasons for doing so:

- It restrains you from making a hasty statement that may not address the question.
- It allows you time to formulate a succinct reply.
- It allows the audience to see you are formulating a thoughtful response.
- It gives value to the question, and to the questioner, by showing that thought is required before answering.

Is it always necessary to repeat or paraphrase a question before answering it?

Not always. If you do so at a small, informal meeting you will sound like a parrot. However, there are advantages in repeating, or possibly paraphrasing, questions when addressing larger audiences:

- It allows the rest of the audience to hear the question.
- It ensures you are going to answer the question posed.
- It allows you time to think about your response.

It is also a useful way to neutralise pejorative questions:

'Why don't you stop polluting our environment?'

becomes

'So you are asking how we can avoid pollution.'

Can you suggest a formula that will help me give strong, memorable, spur-of-the-moment answers?

(S) Formulae have limitations, but the acronym SEER could help you.

(E) Effective responses depend on many things, including the out-come desired by the speaker, the nature of the audience and the context of the question. However, some people may find the acronym SEER useful:

- S = Summary (one-sentence summary statement of your answer).
- E = Elaborate (key point to support your answer).
- E = Example (specific illustration that will make the key point memorable).
- R = Restatement (restatement of summary, using other words).

(E) A chief executive I know was an excellent speaker, but poor at responding to questions. This weakness undermined entire pre-sentations. Then I told him about SEER. It has transformed him. It has given him a thinking format to gather and present ideas in a concise way for maximum impact and recall. His answers, like his speeches, have become strong and memorable.

(R) So while I believe it is always better to communicate in a way that is natural to you, being a SEER could help you think on your feet. After all, if it works for the chief executive, it might just work for you too.

CASE STUDIES

Bernard digs a hole for himself

Towards the end of an induction session Bernard, the director of human resources, is asked why so few senior managers are female. He answers convincingly by explaining how everyone who joins the company has exactly the same chances of rising to the top. There is no glass ceiling here. It is a text-book example of how to answer a potentially damaging question. But he doesn't know when to stop. 'For example,' he goes on, 'look at my case, I started out from a poor family, when I was young. . .' After listening to this long biographical diatribe, the audience has forgotten his key point: namely, that every-one there has the same opportunities. Bernard has neglected the adage: Quit while you are ahead.

Dave doesn't challenge a false presumption

Dave, the sales director of an aircraft company, is asked: 'Since your company is no longer the recognised international leader in the commercial aircraft industry, how can you even attempt to justify. . .?' The initial presumption is wrong; Dave's company enjoys the lion's share of its market. However, he chooses (or neglects) to mention this fact before concentrating on his answer. By failing to contradict the initial assumption, he leaves many members of the audience with the impression that the questioner's statement is true. He should contradict it *before* answering, or perhaps *instead* of answering. 'Oh come now, you know that is not true', before passing on to the next question without dignifying the loaded one with an answer.

Margaret plays it straight

Following a competitive business pitch, Margaret is asked about her company's poor staff retention record. It would be all too easy to go into defensive mode, which would almost inevitably set off a self-justifying ramble. Sensibly she decides to take the positive approach. 'Yes, that is an aspect we want to improve, and this is what we are going to do about it. . .' She gives the impression that she is being fair and honest. This approach wins the day.

SUMMARY

- Maintain control.

- Spell out the ground rules.

- Anticipate and prepare for likely questions.

- Don't allow the session to be hijacked.

- Make sure that each question is clearly understood.

- Hook your answers back to your message.

- Use different phraseology and examples from those in your speech.

- Reserve the right to have the final word.

8
Publicising a Speech

Most people running businesses today are aware of a need to create publicity for their products and organisations. Too few are aware of the need to create publicity for their speeches. You have invested a great deal of time, money and effort in your speech. While the novice may see it as a one-off event, the experienced speaker sees it as one form of many communication opportunities.

This final chapter will briefly explore how to prepare for speech publicity and how to execute it. The purpose is to give you some ideas of how to get maximum exposure for every important speech you deliver. It would take another book to develop this theme fully. Regard this treatment as no more than the start of an enjoyable and rewarding learning process. Let it open your eyes and ears to the many thousands of publicity opportunities that occur in the most unexpected places day after day.

The aim of publicity is threefold:

- to gain attention
- to create interest
- to stimulate desire.

Other than the speech itself, speech publicity opportunities have two places within the speech cycle: *before* and *after* the speech.

BEFORE THE SPEECH

Your object should be to build suspense and interest into your words well before you deliver them.

Sending releases to the media
If you want coverage, you must let the news media know to whom, on what and when you will be speaking. Remember the requirements of each form of media: Newspapers require copy and photos, where appropriate; TV needs brief soundbites of catchy phrases and later

photo opportunities; radio needs simple 15–30 second soundbites, most of which can be read over the phone.

Looking for a human interest angle
People like to know about people. Publicists will question, probe and examine a subject until something unusual comes to light and will build on that until they have a story with human interest as one of the ingredients. So tell them that 'Fifty jobs will be created', not that 'The company will be expanding'.

Finding a local angle
Editors in Wales are unlikely to be interested in an activity in Manchester, but if some Welsh interest could be found then there might be something in it for them ('Manchester brewery to create 50 jobs in Swansea').

Choosing a great title

Speech titles have two purposes: They suggest the general contents of the speech while simultaneously grabbing attention. The more expressive your title, the more attention it will attract. A good title should be:

- Relevant: Don't con your potential audience. A speech entitled 'CJD: a ticking timebomb?' should not be about the cost of cattle feed.

- Intriguing: 'Take a Walk on the Wild Side' is a far more appealing title than 'Country Walks in South Derbyshire'.

- Concise: Make the title punchy: 'The Winds of Change'; 'I have a Dream'; 'Socialism Unbeaten'. The exception is scientific talks, where convention demands long, descriptive titles.

Mailing advance copies to trade magazines

Send a copy of your speech to trade associations. Include a summary or press release highlighting the main points and a few memorable quotes. Three benefits will accrue:

- You will save them time and therefore stand a greater chance of getting publicity.

- You are more likely to be accurately quoted and represented.

- You can make sure your message gets through loud and clear.

Keeping your PR staff informed

Public relations is a method of creating a climate of good opinion in which business can be done. Make sure that your PR staff get one of the first copies of your speech. By using their regular contacts, your staff can build public interest in your speech long before you give it. Further, by having a copy of the draft, they will be better able to answer questions that might arise during the follow-up period.

AFTER THE SPEECH

A speech is like a baby: after delivery it should have a life of its own. To ensure the health and longevity of your words, consider the opportunities that are available for generating:

- in-house publicity
- local and national publicity
- international publicity.

Generating in-house publicity

It is always useful to reinforce messages made to internal audiences. This can be done by:

Having additional copies available

Audiences are most motivated to do something immediately after hearing a dynamic speech than at any other time. Seize the moment by providing copies or summaries of your speech for distribution, not only to the news media but also to the audience itself.

Having reprints made

By having such reprints available, you will be able to hand them out in response to enquiries on the topic, and they can also be used for post-speech publicity. Reprints should be sent to any professional magazines or newsletters in your company's area of interest.

Using excerpts for in-house publications

Don't miss the opportunity to re-use your speech in the company newsletter, magazine or e-mail. Often particular excerpts are especially germane to an internal audience and require little or no writing or thinking – only excerpting.

Generating local or national publicity

The media always needs good material. Help them, as well as yourself, by providing them with some.

Arranging a press conference

A keynote speech will often attract media interest. If you plan to conduct a press conference, you should be sure that you have a public relations specialist with you to manage the event and to keep you from getting in over your head. Your publicist can set the parameters, ward off some questions, encourage and even answer others. A word of caution: If you do open up to the media, don't expect them to stick to issues pertaining to the speech unless you make that clear before you begin the press conference. Otherwise you will get questions on any controversial topic with which you or your company may be associated.

Addressing the media

Many organisations tend to shy away from the mass broadcasting media. The reason for this is not clear, but it may be a feeling that they are not important enough. Never undervalue your worth, especially if there is local interest. There are literally thousands of opportunities out there, so why not write to your local radio or television station? Spell out why the contents of your speech are of interest to their listeners or viewers.

When you are interviewed on radio or TV be yourself at all times, and ensure you state your key points clearly and memorably. In particular:

- don't drink and drivel
- keep your message simple
- continually reinforce your message
- create soundbites
- have a positive attitude
- take and retain control
- don't get drawn into arguments
- cut out *all* jargon
- *converse* with the interviewer (forget the audience)
- use colourful illustrations and examples
- have the last (rehearsed) word.

Television adds complications because you can be seen as well as heard:

- dress naturally but soberly
- don't wear anything that's too tight
- check buttons, flies and zips

- look at the interviewer
- as always, relax and project your personality.

Generating international publicity

Today an important speech can become national or international news in a matter of moments. But even if the media do not beat a path to your door, it is quite straightforward to create your own news and generate international publicity.

The Internet

The Internet changes so rapidly that any listing here would be out-of-date before it is published. However, there are ample publicity opportunities for *all* speech topics. The Net is also valuable for speaker 'chat' rooms and support groups. For an annual fee, the professional speaker can display his wares on one of the many speaker sites.

The BBC

The BBC is most helpful in securing publicity overseas. There are two key access points inside Bush House, London, home of BBC External Services, which includes the World Service. The **export liaison unit** is the first point of contact for good news stories from businesses large and small; and the **facilities unit** provides a daily digest of events for all other departments in the building. They can be contacted at: BBC World Service, Bush House, Strand, London, WC2B 4PB. Tel: (0171) 240 3456. Fax: (0171) 257 8258. E-mail: worldwide.letters@bbc.co.uk. Web site:http://www.bbc.co.uk/worldwide.

The Central Office of Information

There are seven Central Office of Information offices throughout the UK, each seeking news about British business for distribution overseas. As the government's publicity agency, the COI supplies British services overseas with material which reaches people in most parts of the world. Acting on behalf of the Foreign and Commonwealth Office and the British Trade Board, it deploys every medium of publicity except paid advertising to maintain and increase Britain's industrial prestige abroad. The main requirements are for news, pictures, publications or films about the following:

- The launching of a new product, process or service.
- News of substantial new investment.
- The newsworthy opening of a new factory in the UK or overseas.

- A notable success in research or development.
- A large or unusual export order.
- Participation in UK or overseas exhibitions and other promotions.
- Membership of an outward trade mission.
- Visits overseas of senior executives.
- Important overseas visitors.
- The anniversary of a notable invention or achievement.
- Evidence of customers' recognition of a high quality of product.

All accepted material can, if necessary, be treated strictly in confidence until an agreed release date. The COI can arrange to match this date in this country with simultaneous release abroad. This release can be world-wide or in areas specified by the organisation.

QUESTIONS AND ANSWERS

A trade journal wrote a very flattering article about my speech. Can I copy it and send it to my customers?

Legally speaking, no. The article is the copyright of the journal. Ask for permission before you make any large number of copies. Most publications provide a reprint service to cater for just this situation.

I am preparing a press release, and intend to include photographs of myself, our head office and the product we shall be launching next month. What kind of captions should I give the photos?

Captions have two purposes: to *inform* and to *encourage* the reader to look at the story. You should approach the writing of captions with those two points firmly in mind.

not:	Ben Nevis	*but:*	Ben Nevis, Chairman of Matthew and Son
not:	Matthew and Son's head office	*but:*	Matthew and Son's head office at 101 High Street, Anytown
not:	The Tripper	*but:*	The Matthew Tripper mountain bike.

A good way to encourage the reader (or, in the first instance, the editor) is to link the caption to the story:

'In top gear: Ben Nevis, Chairman of Matthew and Son, demon-strates the new Matthew Tripper mountain bike.'

If a particular publication is interested in the topic of my speech, but not sympathetic to my point of view, should I send them a press release or not?

Yes, give them details of your speech. You will not make them more sympathetic by cutting them off from information about your activities.

CASE STUDIES

Ruth publicises the wrong message

Ruth, the chief executive officer of a large public utility, asks her PR section to provide in-house publicity about her forthcoming presen-tation on the benefits of new technology. Unfortunately, she neglects to tell them what central message she wants to convey – and they do not ask. Consequently, the advance publicity merely sparks rumours of mass redundancies. Paradoxically, her message is that new tech-nology will make the utility more competitive, and thereby improve job security.

David targets a hobby-horse

David is a director of a leading chain of DIY stores. He is invited to address his local Chamber of Commerce on 'Ageism in the Workplace'. He knows that the features editor of a certain national broadsheet shares his strong views that ageism should be outlawed by legislation. He tells the journalist about his speech and gains national publicity for his cause.

Charles keeps his words

In 1996 Charles, a computer specialist, began a series of some 20 speeches on various aspects of 'The Millennium Bug'. A year later, he decides that they might form the basis of a book. He spends the next two months re-working his speeches, before submitting a man-uscript to a publisher. This work is accepted and the book published in 1998, providing, inter alia, excellent publicity for both Charles and his company.

SUMMARY

- Publicise your speech *before* you make it.

- Publicise your speech *after* you make it.

- A speech can be delivered over and over again – before the microphone is turned on and long after it is turned off.

A FINAL WORD

The hallmark of an effective speaker is the ability to create value through the transfer of skills, learning and/or enjoyment to an audience. The key is to know precisely what outcome is required, and then to act as the catalyst to provide it.

A message-based framework works well for any business speech. If your material is structured properly, and you have thought carefully about the kind of language you will use, your message is sure to come through loud and clear.

The *way* you present your speech, however, is a personal matter. Coaching does not work. In fact it is counterproductive. You can easily spot a coached speaker. They exaggerate movement and gestures. They overdo eye contact. They insert unnaturally long pauses. They appear to be delivering a soliloquy from *Hamlet*. They artificially laugh – or worse, cry – at something they've obviously rehearsed a hundred times. No one has ever walked away from a speech saying, 'That was the best presentation I have ever attended. His body language was superb.'

Individual style is always the most effective style of communication for speakers, and is universally reassuring to audiences. The challenge therefore is to discover how and why *you* are an effective communicator in a relaxed conversational setting, and then employ this same innate style however daunting and stressful the presentation assignment. It may be hard to accept, but when the pressure is on the answer is to be yourself, not someone else. Your aim therefore must be to reach Stage 4 of the continuum shown in Figure 8.

A Nobel Laureate once told a group of writers standing beside a bar: 'Within a radius of one mile, there are at least a hundred writers better than any of us; the differences between us, as published writers, and them, as unsung geniuses, is only that we have the discipline to *write down* our sometimes quite average books, while they merely *talk about* their possibly great novels.' Do not merely talk

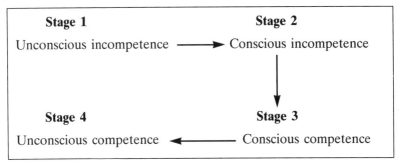

Fig. 8. The road to unconscious competence.

about your literary masterpiece – write it; do not dream of your perfect speech – prepare and present it.

But now the reading must stop and the doing must begin. It is time to put the general precepts of this book into action. Be yourself. Think message. Think audience. Think results. Personal and commercial profit surely will follow.

Glossary

Anecdote. A brief story, often used by speakers to illustrate their point.

Body. The middle of the speech, the section that develops the message and main ideas and supports them with suitable examples, details and illustrations.

Bracketing. A method of linking the conclusion of a speech with its introduction.

Brainstorming. A procedure for generating ideas in which participants use word association. The idea is not to comment on suggestions or make any criticism but to let the imagination flow. The technique can also be practised by an individual.

Conclusion. The last part of a speech, where the speaker's message is re-emphasised.

Connotation. A word's overtones; the special meanings that it carries within a culture.

Content. The environment, surroundings, subject matter or specifics within which processes take place.

Context. The background of the message. The reason you are making the speech.

Credibility. The speaker's believability.

Culture. The specialised lifestyle of a group of people.

Deduction. A process of reasoning whereby a conclusion is derived from a general rule.

Empathy. The emotional effect of imagination which impels a person to assume the identity of another and experience the latter's reactions in some given circumstances.

Feedback. The reaction that the audience gives to the speaker.

Figures of speech. Language that is not meant to be taken in a literal sense. Figures of speech enrich ideas by making them more vivid and easier to visualise.

Five-to-one rule. Every time you hear yourself saying 'I', try to follow it with five 'we's (when addressing an internal audience) or five 'you's (with external audiences).

Goodwill. The audience's perception that the speaker shares their concerns and interests.

Hidden agenda. The ulterior motives or undisclosed reasons behind overt (stated) behaviour.

Hooking an audience. Grabbing their attention.

Identification. The audience's perception that the speaker is similar to them and can be trusted.

Induction. A process of reasoning that arrives at a general conclusion from specific examples.

Inferring. Making generalisations; 'reading between the lines'.

Informative speech. A type of speech that attempts to clarify a concept or process, by defining terms and relationships, or otherwise expanding the audience's knowledge.

Introduction. The beginning of the speech. In the introduction, the speaker attracts the audience's attention, states the topic and purpose, and may preview the main ideas.

Inversion. Turning the normal order of words in a sentence upside-down: 'Ask not what your country can do for you. Ask what you can do for your country.'

Key words. The most important words in a speech.

Message. The central thought or image which is intended to be communicated to another party.

Message-based. An approach to speechmaking based on something you need the audience to know, think or do. It is not a fact.

Metaphor. The application of an imaginary or figurative characteristic to an object or person.

Mind-mapping. A method of planning a speech where you begin with the main idea and branch out as dictated by the individual ideas and general form of the central theme.

Motivation. The reason(s) behind human behaviour.

Narrative. A story or anecdote meant to inform or entertain.

Objective. A specific goal or outcome which can be measured or quantified.

Outcome. The changes in audience attitudes, behaviour or knowledge which are the direct results of a speech.

The Pareto Principle. A rule that states that 80 per cent of what is important is represented by 20 per cent of what exists.

Perception. The process we use to derive meaning from sensory data.

Persuasive speech. A type of speech that attempts to move the audience to action or belief.

Planting (a question). Contriving for a confederate to ask a pre-arranged question.

Prejudice. A preconceived judgement or opinion about a person or group.

Primacy. The tendency for people to remember the first things heard or seen.

Process. A sequence, system, design, model or approach that enables the user to achieve a given, desired result.

Recency. The tendency for people to remember the last things heard or seen.

Rhythm. The choice and combination of words which become music to an audience's ears.

Rhetoric. The art of persuasive and eloquent speech or writing.

Simile. A figure of speech in which one thing (or person) is compared with another.

Theme. A speech's one main idea.

Topic. The subject of a speech.

Transitions. Words that link ideas.

Value-added. The beneficial effect of a speech.

Further Reading

Conceptual Blockbusting, James L. Adams (Penguin).
Creativity and Problem Solving at Work, Tudor Richards (Gower).
Drawing on the Right Side of the Brain, Betty Edwards (Souvenir Press).
Effective Presentation, Antony Jay (Pitman).
Executive's Portfolio of Model Speeches for All Occasions, Dianna Booher (Prentice Hall).
Getting Through! Godfrey Howard (David & Charles).
The Good Publicity Guide, Reginald Peplow (Sheldon Press).
How to Communicate at Work, Ann Dobson (How To Books).
How to Get Your Point Across in 30 Seconds – or Less, Milo O. Frank (Corgi).
How to Master Public Speaking, Anne Nicholls (How To Books).
How to Win Customers, Heinz M. Goldman (Pan Business/Sales).
The Inner Manager, Ron Dalrymple (Celestial Gifts Publishing).
Janner's Complete Speechmaker, Grenville Janner (Century Business Books).
Just Say a Few Words, Bob Monkhouse (Arrow).
The Keys to Creativity, Peter Evans and Geoff Deehan (Grafton).
Lateral Thinking, Edward de Bono (Penguin).
The Magic of Mind Power, Duncan McCall (Gateway Books).
Managing Meetings, Ann Dobson (How To Books).
Mind Mapping and Memory, Ingemar Svantesson (Kogan Page).
One-Liners for Business Speeches, Mitch Murray (Foulsham).
The One Minute Salesperson, Spencer Johnson & Larry Wilson (Fontana/Collins).
Personal Growth and Creativity, Trevor Smith (Insight).
The Presentation Primer, Robert B. Nelson & Jennifer Wallick (Irwin).
Presenting Yourself for Men, Mary Spillane (Piatkus).
Presenting Yourself for Women, Mary Spillane (Piatkus).
The Seven Habits of Highly Effective People, Stephen Covey (Simon & Schuster).
The Strategy of the Dolphin, Dudley Lynch & Paul L. Kordis (Arrow).

The 10 Cornerstones of Selling, Andoni Lizardy (Avant Books).
Training for Decisions, John Adair (Macdonald).
Use Your Head, Tony Buzan (BBC).
Visual Thinking, Rudolf Arnheim (Faber).
Winning Presentations, Ghassan Hasbani (How To Books).
Your Total Image, Philippa Davies (Piatkus).

Index